Factors Affecting the Adoption of the Balanced Scorecard by Small and Medium Sized Enterprises

A Developing Country Perspective

By

Dieu Thuong Ha, Thanh Le and Greg Fisher

Factors Affecting the Adoption of the Balanced Scorecard by Small and Medium Sized Enterprises: A Developing Country Perspective

By Dieu Thuong Ha, Thanh Le and Greg Fisher

This book first published 2023

Ethics International Press Ltd, UK

British Library Cataloguing in Publication Data

A catalogue record for this book is available from the British Library

Print Book ISBN: 978-1-80441-272-5

eBook ISBN: 978-1-80441-273-2

Contents

Chapter 1

Introduction

1.1. Background of the research

Small and medium sized enterprises (SMEs) are considered an important driving force of the world economy since this sector is the biggest contributor to employment in most countries. The sector not only creates a tremendous amount of production but also plays a crucial role in boosting the world economy. Despite being an important component of the economy, SMEs have faced many difficulties in their survival and development (Bach et al., 2021a; Bach et al., 2021b; Bach et al., 2023). Financial constraints limit their resources for implementing big business ideas and long-term investment projects. Lacks training and improving the qualifications of employees affect labor productivity, product quality and market competitiveness of SMEs. Inadequate management skills and business administration methods lead to the failure of the working environment to promote the autonomy and creativity of employees. A large number of SME business owners have not received any basic training, especially in the knowledge about market economy and business administration. Many SMEs are still unfamiliar with building a long-term and sustainable business development strategy with clearly defined goals and missions, specifically for each stage and each condition. To solve these problems, SMEs need to understand how their business is operating, identify where improvements should be made, and have a clear strategic planning process. One way is for them to adopt a performance measurement system (Cocca & Alberti, 2010; Garengo et al., 2005; Heinicke, 2018; Saunila, 2016). Use of a performance management system provides a more complete view of an organization through different measures and perspectives that link together, and enables development of a dynamic system that monitors both internal and external contexts and supports the organization's objectives (Bititci et al., 2000; Kaplan & Norton, 1996; Maas et al., 2016).

Among those common performance measurement systems, the Balanced Scorecard is the most popular and successful system currently in use (Hoque, 2014; Rigby & Bilodeau, 2015; Sorooshian et al., 2016). The Balanced Scorecard was first developed for large companies and has matured in the developed countries (Oghuvwu & Omoye, 2016). The success of the Balanced Scorecard has been enormous, with the adoptions of this model in different organizational types, and in different national and cultural contexts (Aryani & Setiawan, 2020; Madsen, 2015).

> The Balanced Scorecard recently celebrated its 20-year anniversary. Since the Balanced Scorecard was introduced by Robert Kaplan and David Norton in 1992, it has received considerable attention in the management and business community. The Harvard Business Review has referred to the Balanced Scorecard as one of the most influential management ideas of the last 75 years. The consulting firm Bain & Company's biannual survey of management tools and trends consistently ranks the Balanced Scorecard as one of the most widely used tools by managers worldwide. The Balanced Scorecard has also been the subject of much debate in academic circles. In recent years, several literature reviews have been carried out on the extensive Balanced Scorecard research literature. Just in the last few years two special issues of the *Journal of Accounting and Organizational Change* have been devoted to papers on the Balanced Scorecard. (Madsen, 2015, p. 24)

Kaplan and Norton (1996) argued that the Balanced Scorecard could be applied successfully in SMEs. This view has been supported by many researchers all over the world (Cooper et al., 2017; Mahshid Lonbani et al., 2014). Chow et al. (1997) stated that the Balanced Scorecard is an interesting idea that may help SMEs to restructure and survive in difficult times. Birch (1998) suggested that the Balanced Scorecard is as relevant a strategic performance measurement system for SMEs as for blue chip companies. Andersen et al. (2001) confirmed that the Balanced Scorecard is a comprehensive strategic planning method that includes internal and external as well as financial and non-financial aspects that can be used by SMEs to improve their performance. By connecting with the business planning, the Balanced Scorecard is a useful tool for SMEs to develop long-term plans, identify and evaluate risks (Henschel, 2006; Von Bergen & Benco, 2004). Chen and Miao (2010) recommended that SMEs use the Balanced Scorecard to enhance the implementation of knowledge management and to measure its performance. Niven (2011) approved the applicability of the Balanced Scorecard in SMEs and provided a road map for the successful implementation of the Balanced Scorecard in SMEs. Santagada (2012) confirmed that the Balanced Scorecard is a good choice of performance measurement system for SMEs in a competitive environment. It can help SMEs to overcome the challenges and gain significant interest (da Costa Marques, 2012; Kumru, 2012). Aurelia et al. (2018) found that the Balanced Scorecard can support the strategic and operational network management of SME development and success. Malagueño et al. (2018) showed that the use of the Balanced Scorecard brings benefits to SMEs in terms of feedforward control to achieve higher financial performance and exploitative innovation outcomes.

Recently, the use of the Balanced Scorecard in SMEs has spread to Asian countries. Hussin and Yusoff (2013) explained that the Balanced Scorecard could be adapted successfully in Malaysian IT SMEs by developing a simpler model that deals with special characteristics of these companies. Suprapto et al. (2012) indicated four components of the Balanced Scorecard that could be applied in Malaysian Health Care Services SMEs. In Indonesia, most micro enterprise managers agree with the importance of the four perspectives of the Balanced Scorecard in driving the success of the company. They believe the relationships between the perspectives of the Balanced Scorecard are close, and the improvement of one perspective will lead to the enhancement of the others (Sondakh, 2015). Driven by specific features of Chinese SMEs, Yang and Jiehui (2005) created a flexible and adaptable Balanced Scorecard framework with one added perspective of the relationship between financing and government support that could help SMEs run their business better. Chong et al. (2019) indicated that internationalization, including knowledge, trust, commitment, and opportunity development, significantly impacts innovation and the Balanced Scorecard adoption among Malaysian SMEs.

The Balanced Scorecard is a pragmatic model that is extensively adopted in Western and developed countries (Creamer & Freund, 2010; Kasiri et al., 2012; Wu & Chang, 2012). In recent times, it has begun to be adopted in developing countries, especially by SMEs. In Vietnam, as well as other developing countries, the Balanced Scorecard has been proposed as a crucial choice of performance measurement tool for SMEs to guarantee stable growth and a successful future (Tran, 2013). However, there is limited systematic research on the Balanced Scorecard adoption by SMEs. In addition, Norton and Kaplan (1993) stated that there is no standard application model of the Balanced Scorecard. For implementation, it needs to be adjusted for the specific sector (Fernandes et al., 2006). There have been extensive calls for research into the use of the Balanced Scorecard by SMEs in different national contexts. It is necessary to investigate factors that affect its adoption and implementation in order to expand its use for better development and greater profitability of SMEs in developing countries. This research attempts to bridge these gaps in the literature and practice.

This research, in the form of three studies, uses a sequential mixed methods research design to investigate factors that influence the decision to adopt the Balanced Scorecard, the success of the adoption, and the level of adoption by SMEs in developing countries, using Vietnam as a case study context. Obtained results are expected to be applicable to other developing countries of similar development conditions.

1.2. Research and objectives

The overarching problem in the program of this research is to identify important factors that influence the successful adoption of the Balanced Scorecard in SMEs in developing countries. As such, there are three research questions that immediately arise from this research problem:

Question 1: Why have SMEs in developing countries adopted or not adopted the Balanced Scorecard?

Question 2: How do the factors influence the successful adoption of the

Balanced Scorecard by SMEs in developing countries?

***Question** 3:* What are important factors affecting the level of the Balanced Scorecard adoption in SMEs in developing countries?

In an attempt to answer each of the above questions, this book provides a research ready framework that conceptualizes and measures how successful SMEs (in developing countries) are in adopting the Balanced Scorecard. To that aim, this book uses Vietnam as a typical case study for its research.

1.3. Scope of the research

This research focuses on Vietnamese SMEs as representative SMEs in developing countries, in various fields, including manufacturing, trading and services. Different types of ownership are covered, ranging from state-owned and privately-owned enterprises to limited liability, joint-stock, and foreign invested companies.

1.4. Research methodologies

Vietnam is a unique transitional economy that is both manipulated by the market mechanism and regulated by the State with various forms of ownership. To date, the uniqueness of Vietnamese SMEs in this context has not been addressed in research on the Balanced Scorecard adoption. To assess whether previous studies of the Balanced Scorecard in developed countries are relevant to the condition of Vietnamese SMEs, the research in this book applied a sequential mixed method to explore the determinants of its adoption in Vietnamese SMEs. Using mixed method is considered a good research practice as it enables consideration from multiple viewpoints, perspectives, positions and standpoints (Johnson et al., 2007; Mathison, 1988). The initial theoretical framework was constructed from the literature review of earlier studies in the field to provide a better understanding of the problems. Three studies, including two qualitative exploratory studies comprising semi-structured interviews and case studies and a quantitative study comprising a survey, were conducted sequentially to solve the research problems.

1.4.1. Qualitative exploratory studies (Study 1 and Study 2)

The qualitative exploratory studies consisting of interviews (Study 1 included in Chapter 4) and case studies (Study 2 included in Chapter 5) were implemented to refine the preliminary conceptual framework. Study 1, using semi-structured interviews, was conducted to find the reasons why Vietnamese SMEs have adopted or not the Balanced Scorecard. 32 individual interviews were conducted with key informants who were directly responsible for the decision to adopt the Balanced Scorecard in their company. They were either top managers (executives), senior managers (heads of departments) or accountants from SMEs operating in various fields (manufacturing, trading, and services), and in different provinces from the northern areas to the southern areas of Vietnam (from three to six interviewees per company). Template analysis was used to analyze the data to reveal the factors influencing the decision to adopt the Balanced Scorecard in Vietnamese SMEs. The interview protocol for the semi-structured interviews was developed from the literature review and approved by *the Flinders Social and Behavioral Research Ethics Committee.*

Study 2, comprising case studies of four successful Balanced Scorecard adopter Vietnamese SMEs, was conducted to investigate whether and how the impact factors found in Study 1 impacted the successful adoption of the Balanced Scorecard by these Vietnamese SMEs. The four case studies included one in the southern area of Vietnam, one in the north-central, one in the south-central, and one in the northern area. These were selected from the list of the Vietnam Prosperity Joint Stock Commercial Bank (SMEs are the main customers in this bank). All documents including financial statements, bank statements, tax reports, and others that relate to the successful adoption of the Balanced Scorecard in the four case studies were analyzed to provide relevant background information. The in-depth interviews (focus groups or individual interviews) were conducted using a set of topic headings to guide the conversations with the staff involved in the adoption and implementation of the Balanced Scorecard that were introduced by CEOs. There were two focus group interviews with the participants from manufacturing company (case 1) and the transportation company (case 4), and seven individual interviews with Director, Finance manager, Human Resource manager, Business Development manager and Information Technology manager from the software company (case 2) and the agribusiness company (case 3). Case 1 and case 4 preferred to take part in focus group interviews because they had weekly meeting to discuss the Balanced Scorecard adoption in their company. They allowed us to conduct the focus interviews at the time of the meeting to save time. In addition, the participants believed that participating in focus group can help the conversations develop naturally, and the interaction of information between them can help to provide more detailed information. Other participants in case 2 and case 3 chose to take part in individual interviews because they could select the appropriate time and answer the interview questions freely without being influenced by the opinions and views of other participants. The interview protocol was developed from the findings of Study 1 and approved by *the Flinders Social and Behavioral Research Ethics Committee.*

The results of the semi-structured interviews and case studies helped to refine and reinforce the conceptual framework. Taking Contingency theory as the primary theory, the semi-structured interviews and case studies discovered that *top management, organizational strategy, organizational culture, organizational resources, the intensity of market competition,* and *the support of business networks* are the main factors that impact the decision to adopt the Balanced Scorecard and the success of Balanced Scorecard adoption in Vietnamese SMEs. Hypotheses of the relationships between these factors and the level of the Balanced Scorecard adoption in Vietnamese SMEs were developed. The survey (Study 3) was then conducted to test the hypotheses and investigate the factors affecting the level of the Balanced Scorecard adoption in Vietnamese SMEs.

1.4.2. The Quantitative study (Study 3)

The survey in the quantitative study (included in Chapter 6) was then conducted to test the hypotheses about the determinants affecting the level of the Balanced Scorecard adoption in Vietnamese SMEs.

An email survey was used to collect the data. Target informants were top managers of Vietnamese SMEs that had successfully adopted the Balanced Scorecard, in various fields including manufacturing, trading, and services, and in different types of ownership, such as state-owned, privately-owned enterprises, joint stock companies, and joint ventures. This was because these managers have appropriate involvement and knowledge about the adoption of the Balanced Scorecard in their enterprises. These companies were identified from a list provided by the Vietnam Prosperity Joint Stock Commercial Bank, which is a SMEs focused bank. The bank assisted with participant contact and recruitment for this project. From their list of SMEs clients, a representative of the bank contacted approximately 1,500 top managers of SMEs that have successfully adopted the Balanced Scorecard by email. The email asked for their agreement to participate in this research project in a voluntary, and confidential manner, by completing a questionnaire. 222 questionnaires were received, reaching a 14.8% response rate. All of the questionnaires were usable.

The data was analyzed using SPSS statistical software. Test for normality was the first stage of data analysis. This test is used to define whether a data set is well-modeled by a normal distribution and to calculate how likely it is for a random variable underlying the data set to be normally distributed (Ghasemi & Zahediasl, 2012; Greener, 2008). Before testing the theory, it was necessary to assess the reliability and validity of the scale. Cronbach's Alpha method was applied to validate and confirm the unidimensional reliability and internal consistency of the dataset. The Exploratory Factor Analysis (EFA) method helped to evaluate two important types of values of the scale: convergent and discriminant values (Osborne et al., 2008). The EFA method belonged to interdependence techniques and based on the interrelationships. EFA was applied to shorten a set of K variables into a set F (F<K) of more meaningful factors. The basis of this

reduction was the linear relationship of factors with primitive variables (observed variables) (Hair et al., 2019; Hair et al., 1998; Thompson, 2004). Finally, the hypotheses were tested using regression analysis model.

The questionnaire was designed to include information on the Balanced Scorecard adoption in selected Balanced Scorecard adopter SMEs, with specific emphasis on factors affecting the level of its adoption in these companies. The questionnaire consisted of seven pages, including four main parts.

Part 1 included seven questions related the background information in their company.

Part 2 included three questions related the general information of the situation of the adoption of the Balanced Scorecard adoption in their company.

Part 3 included questions related the assessments of respondents regarding six impact factors of the Balanced Scorecard adoption in their company.

Part 4 included questions related to firm performance. These questions asked the respondents to provide the information of their companies' performance after adopting the Balanced Scorecard.

1.5. Structure of book

This book is structured into seven chapters:

Chapter 1	Introduction
Chapter 2	Performance measurement and the Balanced Scorecard
Chapter 3	The Balanced Scorecard adoption in Vietnamese SMEs
Chapter 4	Why have Vietnamese SMEs adopted or not the Balanced Scorecard?
Chapter 5	How do the factors influence the successful adoption of the Balanced Scorecard by Vietnamese SMEs?
Chapter 6	What are the factors affecting the level of the Balanced Scorecard adoption in Vietnamese SMEs?
Chapter 7	Discussion and conclusion

Chapter 1 presents an overview of the research problem, the significance of the research area, and the aims of the research. It also describes the methodology to conduct the research and the structure.

Chapter 2 and Chapter 3 outline the theoretical framework supporting the research and present a review of the literature on performance measurement, Balanced Scorecard, SMEs, and especially Balanced Scorecard adoption in SMEs.

Chapter 4 and Chapter 5 present the results of qualitative research (Study 1 and Study 2). Chapter 4 describes the investigations of the decision of Vietnamese SMEs to adopt or not to adopt the Balanced Scorecard. Meanwhile, Chapter 5 answers the question of how the factors influence the successful adoption of the Balanced Scorecard by Vietnamese SMEs.

Chapter 6 presents the research hypotheses developed from the previous studies and the results of quantitative research (Study 3). It identifies factors affecting the level of the Balanced Scorecard adoption in Vietnamese SMEs.

Chapter 7 discusses the findings along with the theoretical and practical implication of the research. This chapter firstly discusses and draws conclusions from the key findings related to the overall research problem of what factors are influencing successful adoption of the Balanced Scorecard in SMEs in developing countries. Key findings relate to the answers of three research questions: (1) The reasons why SMEs in developing countries have adopted or not the Balanced Scorecard, (2) The way the factors impact the successful adoption of the Balanced Scorecard by SMEs in developing countries, and (3) What factors affect the level of the Balanced Scorecard adoption in SMEs in developing countries. This chapter also outlines the contributions and limitations of this research and suggests items to be included in the future research agenda.

1.6. Conclusion

This chapter provided the reasons for the conduct of this research by presenting the research problem and research issues to be addressed. It then introduced the research methodology and outlined the book. The next chapter provides a comprehensive review of the literature and a description of the context and focus of this research.

Chapter 2

Performance Measurement and Balanced Scorecard

2.1. Introduction

This chapter reviews both the theoretical and empirical literature, related directly to Performance Measurement, the Balanced Scorecard and its adoption by SMEs. It is structured around the research on: (1) performance measurement, (2) the Balanced Scorecard, (3) the Balanced Scorecard adoption by SMEs, (4) Determinants of Balanced Scorecard adoption.

2.2. Performance measurement

What is performance measurement?

Performance is an interesting topic that involves many aspects, such as the establishment, market occupancy, and/or bankruptcy of a company. Performance determines the outputs of certain activities (Rantanen et al., 2007). According to Corvellec (2018), "Performance determines the existence, the nature and the prices of products". Performance is influenced by various internal and external factors of an organization that need to be measured carefully.

To achieve sustainable development, an organization needs to have a relevant performance measurement and lack of a structured performance measurement can lead to failure of a company. Performance measurement plays a critical role in understanding how a business is operating (Bititci et al., 2002; Gunawan et al., 2008; Kaplan & Norton, 1996), and is a central issue in both the literature and in practice (Heckl & Moormann, 2010; Neely, 2005; Richard et al., 2009). Different performance measurement definitions, models, and frameworks have been developed by researchers and practitioners. Neely et al. (1995) defined performance measurement as "the process of measuring the efficiency and effectiveness of action". The definition of performance measurement by Moullin (2003) focused on "evaluating how well organizations are managed and the value the organizations deliver for customers and other stakeholders". Recently, Hatry (2006) defined performance measurement as "regular measurement of the results (outcomes) and efficiency of services or programs". Performance measurement is a structured system that can help an organization get better control and improve the performance by gathering, monitoring and assessing an organization's activities to achieve the planned goals and objectives (Wu, 2009).

Although there are many different views, they all defined performance measurement as a system of management indicators that covers all relevant perspectives of the organization and monitors and drives the organizational strategy to the operational level to communicate that strategy to the entire organization and to its stakeholders. (Hourneaux Jr et al., 2017, p. 150)

The evolution of performance measurement

The evolution of performance measurement can be divided into three periods. The first performance measurement system, developed in the early twentieth century, was an accounting model based mainly on cost accounting to assess the organization's performance. It measured net earnings in relation to cost of operation, not in relation to the firm's total investment in assets, and it concentrated on managing the short-term cost rather than long-term performance (Johnson, 2013). Cost management practices proved incapable of wholly managing cost of products, activities, processes and the cost of quality; it only focused on controlling processes in isolation (Bititci, 1994). Financial measures appeared and gradually replaced the "mission" of the cost accounting model.

Financial measure has dominated performance measurement models in the decades between 1920 and 1980 (Venkatraman & Ramanujam, 1986). This approach concentrated on measuring sales growth, earning per share, profitability such as return on investment, return on sales, and return on equity. In this model, the "market" and "value-based" measurements are more precise than in the cost accounting approach (Hax & Majluf, 1984). Nevertheless, this model focused predominantly on the financial perspective while more comprehensive control of other areas was required (Yadav & Sagar, 2013).

A broader framework of performance measurement with the addition of non-financial indicators has prevailed since the 1980s. The 1990s, in particular, was an era of growing research on management performance as an important approach of management control system. "Within the next five years, every company will have to redesign how it measures its business performance" (Eccles, 1991, p. 617). Under this framework, the performance of an organization is measured more logically and comprehensively. Table 2.1 presents the advantages of Innovative Performance Measurement in comparison with Traditional Performance Measurement.

Traditional Performance Measurement	Innovative Performance Measurement
Based on cost/ efficiency	Value-based
Trade-off between performance	Performance compatibility
Profit-oriented	Customer-oriented
Short-term orientation	Long-term orientation
Prevalence of individual measures	Prevalence of team measure
Prevalence of functional measures	Prevalence of transversal measures
Comparison with standard	Improvement monitoring
Aim at evaluating	Aim at evaluating and involving

Table 2.1 *The evolution of performance measurement. Source: De Toni and Tonchia (2001)*

Many performance measurement frameworks have been designed to meet the demand of organizations to measure their performance. These frameworks have been reviewed and classified in the literature. In their review, Folan and Browne (2005) argued that the Balanced Scorecard system, the Business Process Reengineering Performance Measurement system, and the Medori and Steeple's Performance Measurement system are three valuable examples of performance measurement frameworks. These three models are valuable because they meet the basic requirements of structural and procedural framework for a successful performance measurement system (Folan & Browne, 2005). Yadav and Sagar (2013) examined the research trend of performance measurement frameworks in two decades (from 1991 to 2000, and from 2001 to 2011). They analyzed more than 20 performance measurement systems against the criteria of time and highlighted issues, dimensions of performance measures, contributions, and limitations. The findings of Yadav and Sagar's research showed that the Balanced Scorecard, Performance Pyramid. EFQM – excellence model, and Performance Prism are the dominant performance measurement frameworks. These models have been very popular in the literature as well as in practices because they contribute to the knowledge related to non-financial performance measures, quality, self-assessment and many stakeholders (Yadav & Sagar, 2013).

The literature pointed out that few performance measurement systems have been academically developed (Folan & Browne, 2005). Most popular performance measurement frameworks need to be in practice in organizations a long time. Among the well-known performance measurement systems, the Balanced Scorecard has the reputation as a high-performance measurement framework that adds an integrated strategic perspective to the performance measurement system and fulfills the long-term objectives and vision of the business.

Performance measurement in SMEs

Performance measurement models were first designed and developed for large companies. While the first performance measurement models for large companies appeared in the 1980s, the first research related to SMEs was undertaken nearly ten years later (Taticchi et al., 2010).

Taticchi et al. (2010) showed that more research on SMEs' performance measurement appeared from the beginning of 2000s and developed in two directions: (1) applying the model developed for large organizations to SMEs or (2) designing specific models for SMEs.

The SME sector is a key element not only for industrial development but also for the socio-economic development of every country. However, SMEs always face many challenges in their operation because, amongst other things, the lack of a structured performance measurement can lead these companies to fail. Unstructured performance measures could not only make the achievement of strategic objectives difficult, but could also prevent any strategic development occurring within the company (Hudson, Smart, et al., 2001).

The characteristics of SMEs have been the concern of much research on performance measurement in SMEs. Cocca and Alberti (2010) pointed to the lack of resources in SMEs, including lack of human, managerial time, financial stability, and security, and limitations in skill, all of which lead to poor strategic business planning and human resource management. Moreover, SMEs have to face a highly competitive market and limited customers, which affects the payment of debt and cash flow and results in a lack of control over the future. Garengo et al. (2005) found the main characteristics of SMEs that impact the adoption of a performance measurement model are lack of human resources, inadequate managerial capacity, limited capital resources, poor strategic planning, and misconceptions about performance measurement. The characteristics of SMEs underline the differences between SMEs and large companies. Therefore, a different approach to performance measurement is necessary for SMEs.

> The characteristics of limited resources, limited cash flow coupled with a reliance on few customer, a firefighting mentality coupled with an emphasis on current performance, and potential staff turnover coupled with a flat organizational structure, means that SMEs require an alternative approach to strategic performance measurement development (Hudson, Smart, et al., 2001)

Since 1990s, different well-known performance measurement frameworks have been used as the following:

Accounting and non-accounting measures for quality-based performance in small firms (Noci, 1995) proposes a conceptual framework for choosing most effective models to evaluate quality-related investments in small firms. Specifically, it focuses on the approach that balances different decision needs (completeness, measurability of output, structural characteristics, etc.).

Balanced Scorecard application to SMEs (Chow et al, 1997) provides a framework for SMEs' performance measurement by guiding step-by-step implementation.

Customer orientation and performance (Appiah-Adu and Singh,1998) uses the indicators of new product success, sale growth and return on investment to examine the customer orientation-performance in SMEs and test the possible effects of innovation orientation, market dynamism and competitive intensity on the degree of customer orientation among these firms.

Activity based costing in SMEs (Gunasekaran et al, 1999) provides a framework for implementing the Activity Based Costing (ABC) model in SMEs by reviewing the cost management practices in SMEs and identifying criteria and condition for ABC in SMEs considering the business goals.

Quality model in an SME context (McAdam, 2000) examines how total quality management approaches are applied in SMEs context by a study of 20 SMEs cases.

Computer-based performance measurement in SMEs (Kueng et al, 2000) presents a framework of computer-based performance measurement in SMEs by analyzing SME specific and PM specific criteria.

Performance measurement in the implementation of CIM in SMEs (Marri et al, 2000) proposes a computer-integrated manufacturing framework to improve SMEs' performance by present an empirical study conducted in British SMEs.

Effective performance measurement in SMEs (Hudson, Lean, et al, 2001) presents the limitations of performance measures used in SMEs. By testing through a case study, a new process for developing effective performance measurement in SMEs is proposed.

Indicators for performance measurement in SMEs (Hvolby and Thorstenson, 2001) suggests the Balanced Scorecard approach as a reasonable balanced performance measurement for SMEs. It emphasizes lead-time and lead-time reduction are the primary performance indicators.

Theory and practice in SME performance measurement systems (Hudson, Smart, et al., 2001) evaluates ten performance measurement systems from the literature to find out the appropriate approach for SMEs. A series of interviews with SMEs managers to investigate whether they measure their performance strategically.

Dynamic integrated performance measurement system (Laitinen, 2002) develops a dynamic integrated performance measurement system to measure and improve SMEs' performance. This framework derives from the idea of activity-based costing. It consists of 2 external factors of financial performance and competitiveness and 5 internal factors of costs, production factors, activities, products, and revenues.

A strategic planning model for SMEs based on the Balanced Scorecard (Davig et al., 2004) uses a structured telephone interview with 75 manufacturing SMEs that have fewer than 250 employees. It presents a guideline for SMEs to implement the Balanced Scorecard.

Performance measurements in the implementation of information systems in SMEs: a framework and empirical analysis (Sharma and Bhagwat, 2006) uses a survey methodology to develop a framework for information systems in SMEs to measure and evaluate information system performance in six perspectives: operational efficiency of the information system function, down time of information system, responsiveness of information system, timeliness of information, accuracy of information, and overall competitive position.

Balanced Scorecard implemented in a not for profit SME (Manville, 2007) applies a case based methodological approach exploring the perceptions of two management stakeholder group to discover that the Balanced Scorecard can be implemented within a not for profit SMEs.

Measuring performance of SMEs: the grounded theory approach (Chong, 2008) uses the procedure stipulated by the grounded theory and in-depth semi-structured interviews with the owners-mangers of SMEs to find out how performance is being measured. The findings highlight the equal attention of SMEs on both the financial and non-financial measures.

Performance measurement management for SMEs: An Integrated Approach (Taticchi et al., 2008) proposes a framework for a Performance Measurement Management system design for SMEs by reviewing the literature. This integrated framework overcomes the weaknesses in the previous framework while keeping their strong points.

Supply chain performance measurement framework for small and medium scale enterprises (Thakkar et al., 2009) integrates the main features of Balanced Scorecard and the supply chain operation reference (SCOR) model to develop an integrated performance measurement framework for supply chain evaluation and planning in SMEs.

Development of assessment methodology for improving performance in SME's (Munir Ahmad and Alaskari, 2014) presents a successful and effective assessment methodology for manufacturing SMEs by providing a useful indicator to identify waste and suggesting how such activities could be organized and managed more effectively.

Performance measurement system implementation in a turbulent operating environment (Pekkola et al., 2016) provides a new understanding about the performance measurement design process in SMEs operating in a turbulent environment by revealing the framework for a flexible performance measurement system design.

Performance measurement approach for innovation capability in SMEs (Saunila, 2016) presents a framework to improve the innovation capability through performance measurement in SMEs. The framework assists SMEs to cope with the increasing need for innovation as an asset of their business performance.

Market Orientation and Performance Measurement System Adoption Impact on Performance in SMEs (Länsiluoto et al., 2018) shows the relationship between market orientation, performance measurement adoption and firm performance in SMEs.

In brief, performance measurement in SMEs has received more attention in recent years. More balanced models with financial and non-financial measures have been applied and implemented in SMEs rather than purely financial measures. Among the popular performance measurement systems related to financial and non-financial measures, the Balanced Scorecard has been considered as the most appropriate approach to measure SMEs performance (Andersen et al., 2001; Manville, 2007; Tennant & Tanoren, 2005).

2.3. The Balanced Scorecard

Introduction to the Balanced Scorecard

Before the 1990s, many companies used only financial measures to manage their business and assess their performance (Chavan, 2009). This led to limitations in their management and development because financial measures only report what has happened in the past while enterprises need to have more information for the future (McCunn, 1998). The Balanced Scorecard was proposed by Kaplan and Norton (1992) who included four key perspectives: the Financial perspective, the Customer perspective, the Internal Business Process perspective and the Learning and Growth perspective. These provide a performance management framework by matching "financial measures of past performance with measures of the drivers of future performance"(Kaplan & Norton, 1996, p. 8) that is better in dealing with today's business environment. In the beginning, the Balanced Scorecard was defined as "a set of measures that gives top managers a fast but comprehensive view of the business" (Kaplan & Norton, 1992, p. 71). Over 20 years of development, the concept of Balanced Scorecard has matured beyond being just a performance measurement system, to include roles in strategic management systems and as an organizational communication tool (Basuony, 2014; Cengic & Fazlic, 2008; Niven, 2011).

The Balanced Scorecard is one of the most popular management tools among organizations all over the world (Ax & Bjørnenak, 2005; Mehralian et al., 2017; Sartor, 2019; Sorooshian et al., 2016; Voelker et al., 2001; Watts & McNair-Connolly, 2012). It has been identified as one of the top prevalent management measures for many years (Rigby & Bilodeau, 2009, 2011, 2013, 2015) and has been accepted by thousands of organizations (Kaplan, 2009). Kaplan and Norton's key performance indicators have been applied by around 64% of organizations to evaluate their performance (Kurtzman, 1997). The widespread use of the Balanced Scorecard means it is a topic of great interest in both academic and business communities (Atkinson et al., 1997; Hasan & Chyi, 2017; Hoque, 2014; Nørreklit, 2003; Sartor, 2019).

Organizations have recognized the Balanced Scorecard as a truly necessary management tool (Mooraj et al., 1999), as it solves the problems arising from the sole use of financial measures (Mooraj et al., 1999; Nørreklit, 2003; Otley, 1999) and provides "managers with the instrumentation they need to navigate to future competitive success" (Kaplan & Norton, 1996, p. 2). The Balanced Scorecard is also a feed-forward control system that combines outcome measures and performance drivers together in a cause and effect relationship (De Haas & Kleingeld, 1999; Norreklit, 2000). Anand et al. (2005) concluded the use of the Balanced Scorecard has also led to cost reductions and improvements to the bottom line in organizations.

While the case for the usefulness of the Balanced Scorecard has been widely recognized, it has also received considerable criticism. Critics of the Balanced Scorecard concentrate on the implementation of the concept in practice (Awadallah & Allam, 2015). Butler et al. (1997) found that Kaplan and Norton's concept of the Balanced Scorecard is too general. The design and construction of the Balanced Scorecard has not been well documented, and it can lead to misunderstanding in the conventional accounting sense. Nørreklit (2003) stated that there is a cause and effect relationship between customer satisfaction and loyalty, between loyalty and financial results as suggested by Kaplan and Norton (1992) and Kaplan and Norton (1996), and that the Balanced Scorecard can cause issues in implementing strategic control. Atkinson et al. (1997) criticized the failure of the Balanced Scorecard in connecting stakeholder measures with performance measurement. Brignall et al. (1991), Neely et al. (1995), Maisel (1992), Ewing and Lundahl (1996), and Lingle and Schiemann (1996) opined that the addition of consideration of competitiveness, human resources, employee satisfaction, supplier, and environment could enhance the Balanced Scorecard's framework. Simons (1990) did not support the Balanced Scorecard as a valid strategic control system, because it did not fully explain how strategies are formulated and implemented in organizations.

Despite the debates on the Balanced Scorecard, it has been assessed as the most successful concept in the field of performance measurement, and thousands of public, private and non-profit organizations in all industry sectors and all scales have implemented it (Basuony, 2014; Kaplan, 2009). The publications of Kaplan and Norton on the Balanced Scorecard concept have been the most cited literature sources (De Waal, 2003; Marr & Schiuma, 2003). Hoque (2014) suggested that the Balanced Scorecard will continue to be a crucial organizational control and accountability tool, and will be the valuable option for companies until another advanced innovation device appears. Taticchi et al. (2010) confirmed 30 – 80% of the firms around the world are using the Balanced Scorecard. Aryani and Setiawan (2020) identified seventy-one articles about the Balanced Scorecard topics published in 21 Scopus first-ranked (Q1) indexed journals and found that it continues as a worthwhile performance measurement system. Kureshi (2014) presented the use of Balanced Scorecard as a management tool, as shown in Figure 2.1.

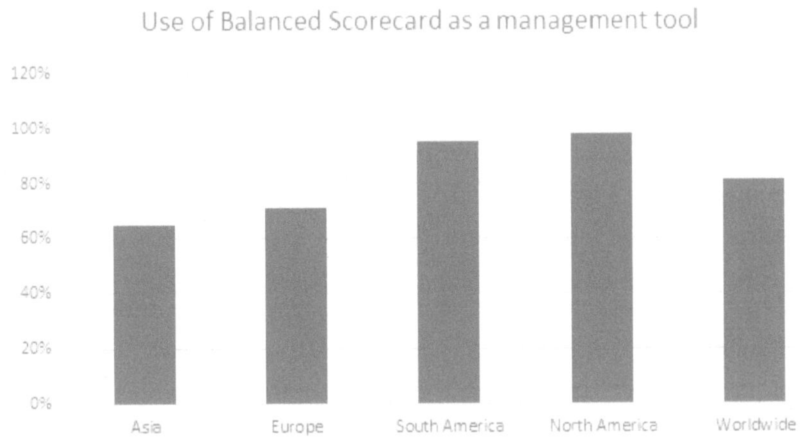

Figure 2.1 *Use of the Balanced Scorecard as a management tool*

The four perspectives of the Balanced Scorecard

The Balanced Scorecard focuses on four main perspectives as shown in Figure 2.2 and is discussed in the following subsections:

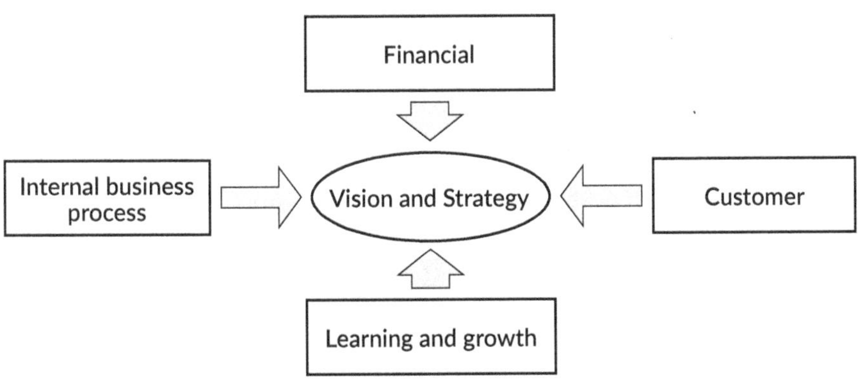

Figure 2.2 *Four perspectives of the Balanced Scorecard*

The *Financial* perspective helps to answer the question of "How do we look at shareholders?". It focuses on long-term objectives of the business by emphasizing profitability objectives and other financial objectives. It can be divided into three stages of the product's life cycle: rapid growth, sustenance, and harvest. In each stage, different financial objectives and strategies are set up. Financial measures, therefore, need to have good design and implementation to keep track of whether objectives and strategies are relevance and promote improvements.

The *Customer* perspective helps to answer the question of "How do customer see us?" Customers play an important role in the development of companies. In the competitive business environment, a company's main mission is to focus on the customer, "To be number one in delivering value for its customers"(Kaplan & Norton, 1992).

The four main concerns of customers in companies are time, quality, performance and service, and cost (Kaplan & Norton, 1992). The Customer perspective needs to determine the objectives of time, quality, performance and service, and cost, which are then translated into specific strategies and measures in order to achieve customer outcomes of market and account share, customer retention, customer acquisition, customer satisfaction, and customer profitability (Kaplan & Norton, 1996).

The main purposes of the Internal business process to support the Customer and Financial perspectives by "delivering on the value propositions of customers in targeted market segments and satisfying shareholder expectation of excellent financial returns" (Kaplan & Norton, 1996).

The *Internal business process perspective* distinguishes the Balanced Scorecard and traditional performance measurement models by exposing two important points. Firstly, while traditional approaches try to control and improve existing business processes, the Balanced Scorecard focuses on recognizing new processes to effectively meet customer and financial objectives. Secondly, the Balanced Scorecard tries to enhance the role of the Innovation process in the Internal business process to reach both short-term and long-term objectives (Kaplan & Norton, 1996).

In the *Learning and Growth perspective,* the infrastructure of an organization is examined with the purpose of achieving long-term growth and improvement based on the three main sources of people, systems, and organizational procedure. The Learning and Growth perspective identifies the objectives of reskilling employees, improving information technology systems, and rearranging organizational procedures, and transfers these objectives into specific strategies and goals. It will help to fix the gaps between the existing capacity of employees, systems, and procedures which have been detected by the three other perspectives of the Balanced Scorecard (Kaplan & Norton, 1996).

Balanced Scorecard evolution

The Balanced Scorecard was first introduced by Kaplan and Norton (1992) as a single performance scorecard model, combining financial and non-financial perspectives (customer, internal business, innovation and learning). The Balanced Scorecard is considered not only as a measurement exercise, but also a performance measurement framework that promotes innovation improvement and help to measure the long-term performance of organizations. Kaplan and Norton have continuously developed their original Balanced Scorecard idea to the present Balanced Scorecard model through several publications.

In Kaplan and Norton's book, *"The Balanced Scorecard: Translating strategy into action"*, (Kaplan & Norton, 1996, p. 9) they renamed and altered two of the four original perspectives. The "Internal business perspective" was renamed the "Internal Business process" with the addition of the "Innovation" component. The "Innovation and Learning perspective" with the addition of "Growth" part and the removal of the "Innovation" element was named "Learning and Growth" (Kaplan & Norton, 1996, p. 9). Further, in this book, Kaplan and Norton developed the Balanced Scorecard from a measurement system to a strategic management system, defining the strategic objectives and demonstrating causality, linking the long-term strategies of an organization to the organization's short-term activities. In addition, the 1996 Balanced Scorecard version stresses the cause and effect relationships among the various measures: "measures of Learning and Growth → measures of Internal Business process → measures of Customer perspective → Financial measures" (Norreklit, 2000).

In their subsequent publications, Kaplan and Norton combined the Balanced Scorecard with management tools in a comprehensive and closed-loop system by focusing on the relationship between the Balanced Scorecard measures and an organizational strategy map (Kaplan & Norton, 2001, 2004, 2008). The strategy map combines strategic objectives within the four perspectives and the causal relationships among them. It presents clearly how tangibles and intangibles assets are converted into tangibles outcomes (Kaplan & Norton, 2001). Through a well-designed strategy map, it is easy to link the strategy and all employees in a company.

2.4. Adoption of the Balanced Scorecard

The adoption of the Balanced Scorecard in general

The Balanced Scorecard, first introduced at the beginning of the 1990s, has been developed over twenty years and has attracted much attention all over the world. A large amount of research related to this topic has been undertaken about different industries (Awadallah & Allam, 2015; Giannopoulos et al., 2013; Hasan & Chyi, 2017) and published in academic, practical, accounting, and management journals and other journals of education, hotel and tourism, and health and public health (Bourne, 2008; Chiu & Li, 2014; De Waal, 2003; Denton, 2005; Madsen, 2015; Magdy Abdel-Kader et al., 2011). Most of these studies addressed the conceptual evolution, adoption and diffusion, implementation and use, performance effects and critical perspectives of the Balanced Scorecard (Hoque, 2014; Madsen & Stenheim, 2015; Phan, 2017). Some of the studies examined the benefits of implementing the Balanced Scorecard (Hoque, 2014), while very few researchers paid attention to it in "strategy mapping", "strategy execution" and "total strategic alignment" (Cheng & Humphreys, 2012). Most studies were case-based and examined the Balanced Scorecard from a single perspective, with little research investigating all its aspects or synthesizing its literature (Magdy Abdel-Kader et al., 2011; Marr & Schiuma, 2003).

An important stream in the research deals with how the Balanced Scorecard is adopted by different organizations, in different national and cultural contexts (Madsen & Stenheim, 2015). Literature shows that 60% of the Fortune 1000 companies in the USA in 2000 and 20% of OECD members in 2003 had adopted the Balanced Scorecard (Grigoroudis et al., 2012; Niven, 2011; Reefke & Trocchi, 2013). Chenhall and Langfield-Smith (1998) found that 88% of investigated Australian firms had experience with the Balanced Scorecard. Further, 24 of the 53 respondent firms in India (approximately 46%) had adopted the Balanced Scorecard (Anand et al., 2005). The proportion of companies that have implemented the Balanced Scorecard all over the world is nearly 70% (Rigby & Bilodeau, 2015). The widest acceptance of the Balanced Scorecard is in the US, the UK, and Northern Europe and there is strong growth of its adoption in South America, the Middle East, Africa and Asia (Rigby & Bilodeau, 2015).

The reasons and benefits associated with the adoption and utilization of the Balanced Scorecard are diverse. Norreklit (2000) argued that the Balanced Scorecard provides a complete image of the company that can be a way to change the communication strategy within the organization. Malmi (2001) identified that the main reasons for its adoption by Finnish firms were to translate strategy into action, to manage organizational changes, to implement quality programs and win quality awards, in response to managerial fads and fashions, and to the abandonment of traditional budgetary control. Juhmani (2007) suggested that the adoption and implementation of the Balanced Scorecard by enterprises gives them a framework for translating the organization's strategic objectives into a collected group of performance measures. In addition, Juhmani (2007) confirmed the Balanced Scorecard also helps companies evaluate their vision and strategy. Bose and Thomas (2007) found that the Balanced Scorecard is being used as a strategic management tool in many companies. Further, Bose and Thomas (2007) confirmed that the learning and growth perspective is very important to strategic management because it allows companies to identify and improve intellectual capital performance. Bisbe and Barrubés (2012) examined the Balanced Scorecard as a management tool in health care organizations and found that these organizations adopt it because they can develop variations to fit each strategic situation. Wanguku (2013) argued that the quality of a firm's control system will be enhanced and its focus can be expanded beyond the analysis of historical financial data when the firm adopts the Basic Scorecard. Jabeen and Behery (2017) concluded that it is an effective model to evaluate and reflect organizational performance and can help to balance the demands of stakeholders and shareholders when they investigate the effect of its adoption in the Middle Eastern context.

Adoption of the Balanced Scorecard in SMEs

The Balanced Scorecard was first designed in large companies and has matured in the developed countries (Oghuvwu & Omoye, 2016). However, Kaplan and Norton (1996) argued that it could be applied successfully to SMEs. This opinion has led to the debate of whether the Balanced Scorecard has the potential to be implemented in SMEs.

It may not always be feasible for SMEs to adopt the Balanced Scorecard approach. Most research has been about large enterprises, which has led to the recognition that the Balanced Scorecard is an effective management tool for organizational performance measurement. Although these findings are valuable, they may not be applicable in the SME context (Bititci et al., 2012). SMEs may lack human or financial resources, be too focused on short-term planning, or have insufficient knowledge to implement the Balanced Scorecard (Ates et al., 2013; Hudson et al., 2001; Johanson et al., 2006; Lonbani et al., 2014). Giannopoulos et al. (2013) showed that most SMEs in the UK and Cyprus are unaware of the Balanced Scorecard. They believe it is irrelevant to SMEs because of their limited resources. They prefer to use financial measures in making the decision rather than non-financial indicators. Kureshi et al. (2009) found that a lack of knowledge about the Balanced Scorecard method was the reason that 61 percent of companies surveyed in Northern Pakistan did not adopt it.

Other researchers discovered incomplete application of the Balanced Scorecard in SMEs (Chimwani et al., 2013; Hanif & Manarvi, 2010; Phillips et al., 2003; Rompho, 2011). SMEs in Nairobi selected only the Financial perspective related measures because of a lack of knowledge about the other three perspectives (Chimwani et al., 2013). Managers in Pakistani SMEs have limited knowledge of the Balanced Scorecard and managed their business dealings based on personal values and customer relationship measures (Hanif & Manarvi, 2010). SMEs in Malaysia, Singapore, Hong Kong and Australia have implemented the Balanced Scorecard, but they have only focused on the finance and customer (Phillips et al., 2003).

However, many researchers support the application of the Balanced Scorecard in SMEs (Cooper et al., 2017; Mahshid Lonbani et al., 2014). Chow et al. (1997) stated that the Balanced Scorecard is an interesting idea that may support SMEs restructuring and surviving in difficult times. Birch (1998) suggested that the Balanced Scorecard is as relevant a strategic performance measurement system for SMEs as for blue chip companies. Andersen et al. (2001) confirmed that it is a comprehensive strategic planning method because it includes internal and external, financial and non-financial aspects that can be used by SMEs for specific strategic purposes, to synchronize strategies with daily works, and to improve performance. By connecting with business planning, the Balanced Scorecard is a useful tool for SMEs to develop long-term plans, identify and evaluate risks (Henschel, 2006; Von Bergen & Benco, 2004). Fernandes et al. (2006) confirmed that the Balanced Scorecard is a significant approach by demonstrating its successful implementation in a case study of UK SMEs. Chen and Miao (2010) recommended that SMEs use the Balanced Scorecard to enhance the implementation of knowledge management and to measure its performance. Niven (2011) confirmed the applicability of the Balanced Scorecard in SMEs and provided a road map for its successful implementation in SMEs. Santagada (2012) proposed that the Balanced Scorecard is a good choice of performance measurement system for SMEs in the competitive environment. It can help SMEs to overcome the challenges and gain significant interest (da Costa Marques, 2012; Kumru, 2012). Aurelia et al. (2018) evaluated how the Balanced Scorecard can support strategic and operational network management by analyzing the successful adoption of a small Italian company. Their findings demonstrate the important role of Balanced Scorecard in the development and success of SMEs.

In recent times, the use of the Balanced Scorecard in SMEs has spread to Asian countries. Based on the specific features of Chinese SMEs, Yang and Jiehui (2005) created a flexible and adaptable Balanced Scorecard framework with the addition of the perspective of the relationship between financing and government support that could help SMEs perform their businesses better. Suprapto et al. (2012) indicated four components of the Balanced Scorecard can be applied in Malaysian Health Care Services SMEs. Hussin and Yusoff (2013) strongly believed the Balanced Scorecard can be adapted successfully in Malaysian IT SMEs by developing a simpler model that deals with the special characteristics of this kind of company. In Indonesia, Sondakh et al. (2017) measured SMEs' performance by using Balanced Scorecard as a measurement tool. They found that these SMEs have good organizational performance, when it is based on the Customer perspective as the highest level of performance and the Financial perspective as the lowest level of performance. Chong et al. (2019) investigated the relationship between the determining factors of internationalization and innovation in the Balanced Scorecard adoption among Malaysian SMEs. They found that the owners and managers of Malaysian SMEs quickly achieve the Balanced Scorecard results if they focus on improving their knowledge, trust, commitment to innovation, and opportunity development.

2.5. Determinant of the Balanced Scorecard adoption

"The Balanced Scorecard is a necessary good for today's organizations" (Mooraj et al., 1999, p. 1). More and more organizations in different sectors want to adopt the Balanced Scorecard as a performance measurement tool to improve their performance. Many authors emphasized that it is important to investigate the variables involved in its adoption. These investigations provide good explanations for why organizations adopt the Balanced Scorecard instead of the other frameworks (Singh & Arora, 2018). Further, they also provide guidance for organizations that want to adopt it to measure their performance.

Malmi (2001) concluded that the logic of the Balanced Scorecard and its supply-side (consultants) has impacted significantly on the decision for adoption by organizations. Radnor and Lovell (2003) suggested three factors that impact on its adoption and implementation. They are: demonstrating its theoretical and practical potential to add service value, obtaining support for its introduction, and not ignoring past experience. Chen et al. (2006) found that the Chief Financial Officer's involvement, participation by different departmental managers, top management support and organization's size are all significantly related to the adoption and implementation of the Balanced Scorecard. Fernandes et al. (2006) specifically investigated how the Balanced Scorecard can be implemented in a case study of a UK SME and found that backing from the Department of Trade and Industry's Knowledge Transfer Partnership Scheme, strong support from top management, good cooperation within departments, and the use of standard hardware and software systems as well as standard e-business specifications are the impact factors of a successful adoption. Braam and Nijssen (2008) examined the empirical evidence of 40 Dutch companies and argued that top management involvement, the influence of the Finance Department, high levels of centralization, and product-market dynamics are the determinants of the adoption of the Balanced Scorecard in Dutch organizations.

On the other hand, De Geuser et al. (2009) found that the adoption of the Balanced Scorecard relates mainly to organizational culture while top management support and the involvement of all employees does not play any role. Wang and Gu (2016) investigated the perceived ease of use, the perceived usefulness, other control systems, manager's evaluation styles and manager's receptiveness to information all impact strongly on the decision of Chinese managers to adopt the Balanced Scorecard. Singh and Arora (2018) tested the perception of 128 Indian bank employees and found out that top management involvement and interdepartmental communication are the two most important impact factors on its adoption. Additionally, their study explored the cause and effect relationship between Balanced Scorecard adoption and employees' behavior, organizational capabilities, and perceived performance.

Chapter 3

The Balanced Scorecard Adoption in Vietnamese Small and Medium Sized Enterprises

3.1. Introduction

The Balanced Scorecard is a pragmatic model that is extensively adopted in Western and developed countries (Creamer & Freund, 2010; Kasiri et al., 2012; Wu & Chang, 2012). In recent times, it has begun to be adopted in developing countries, especially by SMEs. In Vietnam, the Balanced Scorecard has been proposed as a crucial choice of performance measurement tool for SMEs to guarantee stable growth and a successful future (Tran, 2013). However, there is limited systematic research on the Balanced Scorecard adoption by SMEs. In addition, Norton and Kaplan (1993) stated that there is no standard application model of the Balanced Scorecard. For implementation, it needs to be adjusted for the specific sector (Fernandes et al., 2006). There have been extensive calls for research into the use of the Balanced Scorecard by SMEs in different national contexts. It is necessary to investigate factors that affect its adoption and implementation in Vietnamese SMEs in order to expand its use for the better development and greater profitability of SMEs in Vietnam.

This chapter reviews both the theoretical and empirical literature, related directly to the Balanced Scorecard and its adoption by Vietnamese SMEs. The initial conceptual framework supporting the research is also discussed.

3.2. The Vietnamese business environment

A business environment encompasses all factors that affect business decisions such as economic, social, political and technological factors

(Ayyagari et al., 2007). The business environment can push a firm into disaster or create many opportunities for potential market exploitation. Therefore, having a good understanding on the business environment will help companies succeed in their conduct of business, open new avenues, develop dynamism in their approach, and create opportunities for growth and control over environment (Bigsten & Söderbom, 2006; Bourgeois, 1980; Maruichi & Abe, 2018). In particular, the business environment has a strong impact on the establishment of new firms (Klapper et al., 2004).

Vietnam is located in South East Asia with a current population of 97.3 million people.[1] Vietnam is known as a new rapidly emerging center of economic growth in South East Asia that attracts foreign investors because of the large number of potential consumers and low production costs. Vietnam is a driving force of the development and integration of the Greater Mekong Sub-region and a member of the Association of Southeast Asian Nations (ASEAN). In addition, Vietnam has been well known as a successful country in transition to a market economy with a high concentration of SMEs. The history of Vietnam's economy can be divided into two main periods: before and after Doi Moi (Innovation).

Before Doi Moi

Before 1975, Vietnam had suffered from Chinese and French domination for a long time, and also 30 years of warfare known as the Vietnamese War against the Americans. In this period Vietnam's was a laggard agricultural economy. After the reunification from 1975 to 1986 Vietnam's economy followed the centrally planned model of the former Soviet Union and other socialist countries with the economy managed by the government from top to bottom (Doan, 2012; Nguyen, 2016). In this model, the government plans and controls all economic activities from production targets, capital, material to labor, wages, product prices; heavy industry is prioritized in the industrial sector; cooperatives are the sole economic unit in the agricultural sector that produce agricultural and food products with targets assigned directly

1 https://worldpopulationreview.com/countries/vietnam-population/

by the government (Nguyen, 2016). However, this kind of economic model was inefficient; it led to the multiyear economic crisis, and the annual inflation was up to 776% (Tran et al., 2007). Vietnam's economy in this period needed to undergo a comprehensive reform.

After Doi Moi

At the end of the 1980s, Vietnam launched an economic reform program. This reform featured innovation in economic thinking and economic management mechanisms to create socio-economic stability and raise the living standards (Government of Vietnam, 1988). Since then, the country has been transformed from a centrally planned to a market-oriented economy. In this model, the expansion of private enterprises, that began to be considered as a crucial force for the economic development and growth of the country, was promoted by a more open and transparent business legal system, and entrepreneurs and SMEs were free to set the quantities and the prices of their products based on the market mechanisms. Moreover, Vietnam joined the international market by becoming a member of regional and international organizations such as WTO, APEC, and ASEAN. Keeping Vietnam's economic growth on track requires significant improvements by different elements of society, especially by the Vietnamese government. Hansen et al. (2009) stated that Vietnam experienced government intervention and support, especially in the business environment. Later, the Vietnamese government enacted the 2013 constitution, the 2014 enterprise law, investment, and the 2013 tendering law. The resolutions providing details to these laws were also published: the 30C/NQ-CP resolution focuses on Administrative Reform program in 2011 – 2020 period; the 19-2014/NQ-CP resolution, the 19-2015/NQ-CP resolution and the 19-2016/NQ-CP resolution focus on missions and solutions in business environment improvement and competitiveness index enhancement until 2020. The Vietnamese business environment has become more competitive and transparent. Vietnam has become known as one of the Asian countries with a good business environment. It was ranked 82/190 good business environments in the world in 2017, which was an increase of nine levels from 2016 (Doing Business Report 2017). The United Overseas Bank's Asian

Enterprises Report 2016 assessed Vietnam as one of the most popular expansion destinations in Asia, following Singapore and Japan, because of its stable political environment and favorable economic conditions with low inflation and an accommodative monetary policy as well as a young and active workforce (United Overseas Bank's Asian Enterprises Report 2016). The development of Vietnam has been assessed one of remarkable progress with important economic growth and sustainability, foreign trade expansion, and fast poverty reduction (Calza et al., 2019; Maruichi & Abe, 2018; Tenev et al., 2003; Tran et al., 2007).

3.3. SMEs in Vietnam

After *Doi Moi,* SMEs have become the main economic sector to contribute significantly to the Vietnamese socio-economic successes. The development of SMEs is considered as one of the key impact factors on the successful transition (McIntyre, 2003; Vuong et al., 2019).

Definition of SMEs in Vietnam

The World Bank report in 2015 stated that SMEs are the most common businesses found across the world's economies (World Bank, 2015). They occupy more than 90% of companies in most countries and contribute between half and three-quarters of the value added to the economy. They also contribute significantly to employment. According to the World Bank's investigation, 600 million jobs will be needed in the next 15 years for the growing global labor force, and most of them are for SMEs. In the United States, SMEs are considered the backbone of the US economy. They make up 99% of all firms, employ more than 50% of private sector employees and create 65% of net new private sector jobs. SMEs are also dominant in exports: they represent 98% of all US exporters and around 35% of US export revenue (Firoozmand et al., 2015). Across the EU28, about 23 million SMEs (occupying 99.8% of all enterprises) generated 3.9 trillion Euro (equal to 57.4%) in value added and employed 90 million (equal to 66.8%) workers in 2015 (Annual Report on European SMEs, 2015).

In East Asian countries, SMEs have been recognized as the priority area. They contribute 30-60% of GDP and create more than 50% of value added or sales on average; they also take 30% of total exports from APEC economies (Tran & Charles, 2016). In the East Asian financial crisis of 1997, SMEs played a crucial role in the countries' sustainable recovery because SMEs recovered from the crisis more easily than large companies.

In Vietnam, SMEs were first defined in the Government Decree No.90/2001 CP-ND on supporting the development of SMEs as "small and medium enterprises are those independent business and production establishments that have registered their businesses under the current legislation, have the registered capital of less than VND 10 billion or have an average number of annual employees of less than 300". According to this decree, SMEs can be defined based on the two criteria of capital and number of employees or on one of the two because of the specific socio-economic situations of sector and locality.

However, in their processes of operation and development, SMEs in different fields of business have specific standards. To detail the criteria of SMEs in each sector, the Government Decree No.56/ 2009 CP-ND on assistance to the development of SMEs that supersedes Decree No. 90/2001/ND-CP defined SMEs as businesses that have business registration in accordance with the law, are divided into three levels: micro, small and medium scale total capital (total capital equivalent to total assets is determined in the balance sheet of enterprises) or number of employees per year (total funding is the priority criteria). This official definition is the basis of almost all Vietnamese ministries and agencies' investigations, annual syntheses, and statistical publications on SMEs (Le, 2017). Criteria of Vietnamese SMEs are identified as presented in Table 2.3:

Sector	Very small enterprises	Small-sized enterprises		Medium-sized enterprises	
	Number of laborers	Total capital	Number of laborers	Total capital	Number of laborers
I. Agriculture, forestry, and fishery	10 persons or fewer	VND 20 billion or less	Between over 10 persons and 200 persons	Between VND 20 billion and VND 100 billion	Between over 200 persons and 300 persons
II. Industry and construction	10 persons or fewer	VND 20 billion or less	Between over 10 persons and 200 persons	Between VND 20 billion and VND 100 billion	Between over 200 persons and 300 persons
III. Trade and service	10 persons or fewer	VND 10 billion or less	Between over 10 persons and 50 persons	Between over VND 10 billion and VND 50 billion	Between over 50 persons and 100 persons

Table 3.1 *Criteria of Vietnamese SMEs in different sectors (Government Decree No.56/ 2009 CP-ND, 2009)*

Most recently, the Government issued Decree No. 39/2018 / ND-CP detailing several articles of the Law on Small and Medium Enterprises Support, including criteria for identifying small and medium enterprises as presented in Table 2.4, 2.5, and 2.6.

Sector	Number of laborers	Total of turnover	Total of capital
Agriculture, forestry, and fishery	No more than 10 people	No more than 3 billion	
Industry and construction			
Trade and service		No more than 10 billion	No more than 3 billion

Table 3.2 *Criteria of Vietnamese SMEs in different sectors (Government Decree No.39/ 2018 ND-CP) - Very small enterprises*

Sector	Number of laborers	Total of turnover	Total of capital
Agriculture, forestry, and fishery	No more than 100 people	No more than 50 billion	No more than 20 billion
Industry and construction			
Trade and service	No more than 50 people	No more than 100 billion	No more than 50 billion

Table 3.3 *Criteria of Vietnamese SMEs in different sectors (Government Decree No.39/ 2018 ND-CP) - Small enterprises*

Sector	Number of laborers	Total of turnover	Total of capital
Agriculture, forestry, and fishery	No more than 200 people	No more than 200 billion	No more than 100 billion
Industry and construction			
Trade and service	No more than 100 people	No more than 300 billion	No more than 100 billion

Table 3.4 *Criteria of Vietnamese SMEs in different sectors (Government Decree No.39/ 2018 ND-CP) - Medium enterprises*

The status of Vietnamese SMEs

As 97% of all Vietnamese enterprises, SMEs make essential contributions to the reduction of the unemployment rate, elimination of poverty, and creation of social stability. They add 33% of total State budget revenues, 49% of created added value for the economy and 41% of GDP, narrowing the development gap among localities of Vietnam (Can, 2017). Also, SMEs play an important role in helping Vietnam overcome the "shocks" in the period of transformation from a centrally planned to a market-oriented economy and the collapse of the Socialist bloc in Eastern Europe (Le, 1997). At present, according to the Vietnam General Statistics Office, there are more than 500,000 operating SMEs.

The rapid development of Vietnamese SMEs has been supported

strongly by business environment reforms, in the form of many specific policies and programs from the government and international organizations. The government concentrated on creating an equal business environment for SMEs and adding the SMEs sector into the wider economy. In 2001, the government started to pay official attention to supporting the development of SMEs by publishing the Decree No.90/2001 CP-ND. From 2006 to the present, many decrees have been published. For example, Decree No.236/2006/QD-TTg supports SME development in the period of 2006-2010; Decree No.56/2009 CP-ND replaces Decree No.90/2001 CP-ND to continuously support SME; Decree No.1231/2012/QD-TTg presents the solutions and programs in support of SME development, including financial supports, market supports, human resource development supports, and policy supports; the most recent Decree: Government Decree No.39/ 2018 ND-CP details a number of articles of the Law in Small and Medium Enterprises Support.

In addition, Vietnamese SMEs also received support from many organizations. Examples are the SME Promotion Agency for SME development, provincial departments of planning and investment, sector-focused government agencies, business associations, private business development service providers and financial institutions, and universities and research institutions (Tran et al., 2007).

CIEM (2016) confirmed that the Vietnam business environment for SMEs has improved. In comparison with the 2013 survey, the amount of job creation by SME increased by 5.2% while the annual number of bankrupt SMEs decreased by 8.2% and the number of new SMEs increased rapidly. The ability of SMEs to access capital resources has developed; in 2011, 45% of surveyed enterprises could not access official capital but by 2015 this figure dropped to only 24%. However, constraints and challenges to Vietnamese SMEs' development remain lack of capital, ineffective development policies, and limited business ability. Many SMEs cannot borrow money from banks because they do not have collateral. Consequently, that they cannot invest in technology, production, and market expansion etc. Further, the education level of SMEs' managers is not too high. With over 50% lacking tertiary education, they cannot access to modern management theories and experiences. Furthermore, the high rate of income tax for SMEs at 20% and many additional unofficial costs set up SMEs to fail. Tran (2015) stated that Vietnamese SMEs are dealing with four main limitations: low understanding of the law, difficulty in the consumer market, a highly competitive environment and being negatively affected by the economic crisis.

The Balanced Scorecard in Vietnamese SMEs

Applying a modern performance measurement system is a good way for Vietnamese enterprises, especially for SMEs to enhance their competitive ability (Le, 2017; Pham & Bui, 2015). Using the performance measurement system will improve SMEs' decision-making processes, management processes, and strategic control (Andersen et al., 2001; Garengo et al., 2005). Eurocham (2011) suggested the Balanced Scorecard as a useful management tool to create a strong strategic management capacity a long-term vision and a well-formulated strategy for Vietnamese business associations.

The Balanced Scorecard was first introduced into Vietnam at the beginning of the 2000s (Tran, 2012). However, at that time Vietnamese managers, and Vietnamese academics were not as interested in it as businesses and academics in other countries. According to VNR 500 (2009), only 7% of Vietnamese companies were using the Balanced Scorecard, with a further 36% intending to use it and 57% having no plan to use it. Greater interest in adopting and implementing the Balanced Scorecard in Vietnamese organizations arose after Kaplan, one of the Balanced Scorecard's designers, visited Vietnam in 2011. In 2015, a Vietnamese Balanced Scorecard private sector organization-Balanced Scorecard Vietnam, a member of the US Balanced Scorecard Institute, was established. Since then, scholars and managers have started to focus on the use of the Balanced Scorecard in SME and a number of seminars and workshops have been held (Pham & Bui, 2015) .

According to Bui (2009), Vietnamese SMEs can implement the Balanced

Scorecard if they focus on the perceived benefit for the organization, its perceived usefulness, and with a positive attitude. Pham and Bui (2015) compared SME adopters and non-adopters of the Balanced Scorecard and found that the adopters were the more stable and developed SMEs. Nguyen (2017) confirmed the feasibility of the Balanced Scorecard implementation in Vietnamese SMEs.

Recently, the role of the Balanced Scorecard in Vietnamese SMEs' performance measurement has increased. Vu et al. (2018) found that it is a relevant performance measurement model for Vietnamese garment SMEs to improve their performance. Vuong (2018) confirmed the contribution of the Balanced Scorecard in the performance of Vietnamese manufacturing SMEs with findings that organizational commitment, business planning, controlling, and strategy implementation are the main factors impacting the performance of Vietnamese manufacturing SMEs.

The Balanced Scorecard has been proposed as a crucial choice of performance measurement tool for Vietnamese SMEs to guarantee a stable growth and successful future (Tran, 2013). However, Norton and Kaplan (1993) emphasized that there is no standard application model of the Balanced Scorecard. To implement the Balanced Scorecard each company must adapt to their mission, strategy, technology, and culture. It is necessary to discover factors that affect the adoption of the Balanced Scorecard by Vietnamese SMEs in order to achieve its widespread use in Vietnam.

Determinants of the Balanced Scorecard adoption in Vietnamese context

The adoption and implementation of the Balanced Scorecard in the Vietnamese context have been considered in literature and practice. More researchers are investigating the determinants to discover good solutions for its adoption in Vietnamese enterprises. Tran (2012) found that the level of involvement of top managers, the power of the finance department, internal communication, product dynamics, and standardization all have a positive relationship the in Vietnamese context with adoption in organizations. Trinh (2014) suggested that top leader's viewpoints, strategic planning and execution, performance assessment, human resource capacity, and operational management are factors that impact on its adoption in Vietnamese enterprises.

In 2018, three research projects were undertaken to investigate determinants of the adoption of the Balanced Scorecard in Vietnam. Vo and Pham (2018) conducted a study of 147 listed companies in Ho Chi Minh using a mixed-methods (qualitative and quantitative) approach, to examine the effect on its implementation of the size of company, management perception, business strategy, company culture, the Balanced Scorecard operational expense, and accountants' capabilities. Nguyen (2018), using the case study method, examined the implementation of the Balanced Scorecard in a Vietnamese organization, and found three phases of initiation, execution, and operation and three mechanisms of communication, training, and institutionalization impact adoptive management innovations, including adoption of the Balanced Scorecard. Nguyen (2018) found that in each phase, a series of flexible and suitable mechanisms are necessary for the effective adoption of management innovation. Dinh et al. (2018) tested the relationship between contingency factors and Balanced Scorecard implementation by surveying 217 firms in Vietnam. The findings showed that the intensity of competition, total quality management, the business strategy, and perceived environment uncertainty have important positive effects on its adoption.

The determinants of the Balanced Scorecard adoption in Vietnamese SMEs seem to be under-researched. Bui (2009) identified three important determinants for organizations deciding to apply the Balanced Scorecard including the perceived benefits to the organization, ease of use of the instrument, and importance of a positive attitude of management. Pham and Bui (2015) explored three factors including the positive adoption of innovation, management by objectives, and advanced technology in Vietnamese SMEs and found that businesses engaged in these three factors were likely to be able to successfully adopt the Balanced Scorecard. From the literature review of Balanced Scorecard adoption in Vietnamese SMEs, Nguyen (2017) found that top management plays a very important role, including top management knowledge and experiences of the Balanced Scorecard. Ta (2019) discovered six factors that impact the adoption of the Balanced Scorecard in SMEs. They are (1) firm size, (2) organizational strategy, (3) Balanced Scorecard awareness of business owner, (4) the cost of the Balanced Scorecard adoption, (5) ease of the Balanced Scorecard use, and (6) the benefits of the Balanced Scorecard use.

Theory driven research

Contingency theory

Recently, many researchers have adopted Contingency theory as a theoretical framework for their research on the factors influential on the adoption and implementation of performance measurement systems and the Balanced Scorecard (Chenhall, 2003; Hendricks et al., 2012; Quesado et al., 2016). Islam and Hu (2012) defined Contingency theory as

> Contingency theory is an approach to the study of organizational behaviour in which explanations are given as to how contingent factors such as technology, culture and the external environment influence the design and function of organizations. (Islam & Hu, 2012, p. 5159).

Contingency theory argues that there is no common relevant application of control system in organizations. The control system depends on contingency factors surrounding organizations (Otley, 1980). According to Fakhri (2012), there are three main reasons for the use of Contingency theory in current papers: (1) the contingency framework offers reasonable explanations for different applications of performance measurement systems, (2) Contingency theory provides the best logical analysis, (3) the contingency framework is an empirical framework that permits research to develop relevant hypotheses, and analyze the selected factors statistically.

Contingency theory has been reviewed as a theory of management accounting and control since the 1970s (Otley, 2016). In 2003, Chenhall (2003) argued in support of using the Contingency theory in the exploration of impact factors on the adoption of management accounting systems. Since then, the Contingency theory has been used in theory driven research on the impact of contingent variables on the adoption and implementation of performance measurement systems, including the Balanced Scorecard (Ahmad & Zabri, 2015; Cardoso Vieira Machado, 2013; Chenhall, 2003; Fakhri, 2012; Garengo & Bititci, 2007; Hendricks et al., 2012; Hoque & James, 2000; Liu et al., 2014; Oghuvwu & Omoye, 2016; Quesado et al., 2014, 2016; Speckbacher et al., 2003). Based on this theoretical framework, research has progressively identified the factors impacting the decision to adopt or not adopt performance measurement systems and the Balanced Scorecard.

Oghuvwu and Omoye (2016) stated that the adoption of the Balanced Scorecard from the viewpoint of Contingency theory depends on the organization's situation. Quesado et al. (2016) used the Contingency theory as a relevant framework for their research on the determinants of the adoption of the Balanced Scorecard in organizations. Hoque and James (2000) used Contingency theory to search for the relationship between three impact factors, (organization size, product life-cycle stage and the strength of market position), and the use of the Balanced Scorecard. Liu et al. (2014) applied the Contingency theory perspective to examine the impact of four contingent variables on the Balanced Scorecard adoption in the context of Singaporean manufacturing firms. They found that these contingent variables have a significant influence on the results of its adoption. Hendricks et al. (2012) confirmed the role of the contingency framework in examining the importance of contingent variables of firm size, strategy type, environmental uncertainty, investment in intangible assets, and prior performance in finding the reasons of organization's decision to adopt the Balanced Scorecard.

"The contingency approach to management accounting is based on the premise that there is no universally appropriate accounting system which applies equally to all organizations in all circumstances" (Otley,

1980, p. 413). Thus, following the assumptions of the Contingency theory, the adoption of the Balanced Scorecard by an organization depends on different situations in the external and internal environments of the organization. This literature review confirmed that through the lens of Contingency theory, research on determinants of the Balanced Scorecard adoption in Vietnamese SMEs can be investigated appropriately. Contingency theory will provide a referent theoretical framework to describe the contextual, internal, and external impact factors on the adoption of the Balanced Scorecard by Vietnamese SMEs.

Initial conceptual framework

This present research deals with factors affecting the adoption of the Balanced Scorecard in SMEs operating in Vietnam. As a starting point, the Contingency theory is used as the theoretical framework because of its wide use in management accounting. From the review of theoretical and professional literature, firm size, external environment, culture, leadership, ownership, and strategy are the contingent factors found in many studies of determinants of performance management and Balanced Scorecard adoption. They may also be relevant in the Vietnamese SMEs context. Therefore, this present research included these factors in the initial conceptual framework to find out the determinants of successful Balanced Scorecard adoption in Vietnamese SMEs.

Leadership

Managers, especially top managers, generally are the most influential people an organization's decision-making, strategy, design and management system; in other words, "the organization is a reflection of its top managers" (Hambrick & Mason, 1984). Kennerley et al. (2003) found that leaders have the main responsibility to choose the relevant performance measure for their organization and to ensure the effective operation of this system. Challis et al. (2005) showed that leaders create a culture that attracts different groups within an organization to cooperate in the main mission of the organization. Braam and Nijssen (2008) argued that top management involvement supports the confident adoption and implementation of the Balanced Scorecard in businesses.

In the SMEs sector, Thong and Yap (1995) found that the owner/manager is a symbol of the company, and plays an important role in deciding the company's innovation. Lybaert (1998) found that the owner/manager of a SME is the main decision maker in the development of management accounting practices. Al-Omiri (2003) confirmed the close relationship between top management and successful ABC implementation in SMEs. Ahmad and Zabri (2015) found that the commitment of owner/manager is a contingent variable significantly influencing the implementation of a budgeting system, the decision support system and the strategic management accounting in SMEs. Volery et al. (2015), and Glaser et al. (2015) found that owner/managers are the key person in all exploratory projects about SMEs.

The literature and empirical research supported the vital impact of leadership on the adoption of innovation and specifically on the adoption of management measures (Braam & Nijssen, 2008; Hambrick & Mason, 1984; Hendricks et al., 2004; Murphy & Southey, 2003). Top and senior management involvement are considered the main components of the leadership factor that decide on successful adoption of the Balanced Scorecard in an organization (Bisbe & Barrubés, 2012; Chan, 2004; Inamdar et al., 2002).

External environment

The external environment of an organization includes all outside factors, situations, conditions, and other related issues that can affect its operation. According to Contingency theory, an organization may adopt and use a performance management system because of its environmental circumstances (Chenhall, 2003). This system will be continuously adjusted to fit the company's environment to help the company manage and measure its performance.

Kaplan and Bruns (1987) argued that competition is the most important external environmental factor encouraging a manager to apply a new cost system to an organization. Luther and Longden (2001) found that the intensity of market competition is the reason for the change in management accounting in South Africa. Abdel-Maksoud et al. (2005) confirmed the relationship between the intensity of market competition and use of performance measurement systems. They showed that companies facing difficult competitive conditions tend to adopt multidimensional management measures to manage their performance. Ahmad and Zabri (2015) corroborated the positive influence of the intense market competition on performance measures use, as was confirmed in much previous research (Abdel-Maksoud et al., 2005; Chenhall & Morris, 1986; Mia & Clarke, 1999).

In addition, the support of local government could be considered as an important external environmental factor impacting the adoption of a performance measurement system by SMEs. Roxas et al. (2009) confirmed the significant role of local governments in SMEs' strategy implementation. In emerging countries, local governments contribute significantly by creating policies that are clear and by providing convenient information for SMEs (Bertolini & Giovannetti, 2006; Meyer & Nguyen, 2005; Tran et al., 2009). Local governments not only impact firm performance, but also push firms toward strategic approaches that are more effective in operation. Nguyen et al. (2018) suggested the importance of the role of government in the performance of firms in countries that have a history similar to Vietnam's. Historically, Vietnam was divided into two parts: the northern and the southern regions. This type of context could lead to the different management features of the local governments, such as freedom from corruption, administration transparency, and proactivity in planning and implementing business policies in one area and the contrasting features in the other. Such management features were found to be important determinants of SME's performance.

Firm size

Size of firm has been considered as one of the main factors affecting the way that an organization designs and uses a management measure (Ahmad & Zabri, 2015; Burns & Stalker, 1961; Chenhall, 2003; Fakhri,

2012; Hendricks et al., 2012; Hoque & James, 2000; Lawrence & Lorch, 1967; Liu et al., 2014; Oghuvwu & Omoye, 2016; Quesado et al., 2016; Speckbacher et al., 2003; Vo & Pham, 2018; Woodward, 1980). Bruns and Waterhouse (1975) proved that while SMEs prefer a flexible "Interpersonal Control Strategy" based on individual connections, larger companies manage their organizations following an "Administrative Control Strategy" with formality and standard. Merchant (1981) showed that size of the organization could decide the control strategies. Widener (2006) found that the large companies are more likely to use multiple performance measures than SMEs. Taylor and Taylor (2014) showed that the impact of firm size on the adoption of a performance measurement system should be considered for four main reasons: (1) Researchers in this field have suggested that the size of firm is relevant; (2) Contingency theory supports the view that firm size affects the effective application of a performance measurement system in businesses; (3) Some studies of performance measurement practices, such as TQM, Lean and CSR, were approved as the empirical evidence of the significant relationship between firm size and performance measurement implementation; and (4) The effects of firm size on performance measurement system are under-researched. The bigger a company is, the more complicated communication and monitoring issues are. Companies of a bigger scale are more likely to adopt a complex management model to manage their operations. The Balanced Scorecard is a relevant system for completion of a business's requirements (Kooke & Muturi, 2015). Hoque and James (2000) suggested that firm size, including revenue, total assets, and number of employees, impacts significantly on the design and usage of management models.

Organizational culture

Culture can be understood as a group of beliefs, values, sets, communications, and behaviors which impact people. Organizational culture is a combination of values and behaviors that shape organizational achievement (Chenhall, 2003). Baird et al. (2004), and Chia and Koh (2007) confirmed that the contingent variable of organizational culture impacts management accounting and control practices. Henri (2006) found that culture can impact all activities of the company, both in interactions and functions. Perera et al. (2007) showed that the absence of innovation-oriented organizational culture can lead to the limitation of the use of the Balanced Scorecard in councils. Asiaei and Jusoh (2014) argued that culture is obviously a vital factor impacting the use of multidimensional performance measurement systems. A company with an innovation-oriented culture tends to use a multidimensional performance measurement system to a greater extent than others. Kumar (2001) and Robbins (2006) suggested the following main characteristics of an organizational culture: innovation, attention to detail, team orientation, and outcome orientation. Such cultural types promote highly structured networks of communication (Burns & Stalker, 1961).

Organizational strategy

Organizational strategy exerts a vital impact on the design, adoption and diffusion of the innovation process (Chenhall, 2003; Dinh et al., 2018; Fakhri, 2012; Garengo & Bititci, 2007; Hendricks et al., 2012; Liu et al., 2014; Vo & Pham, 2018). Koufteros et al. (2005) and Sila (2007) found that strategy is one of the important contingent factors impacting an organization's ability to achieve high performance levels. A good organizational strategy undertakes the process of implementation sequentially from formulating the strategy to deploying it in the whole company, helping all members of company to get involved in the process. "The realized strategy is one that emerges from the bottom, from the set of innovation and change initiatives that are undertaken day after day" (Garengo & Biazzo, 2012, p. 84).

Gosselin (1997) found that strategy influences the extent of adoption of activity-based costing in organizations. Hoque (2004) found a significant relationship between strategy and adoption of non-financial measures in organizations. Cadez and Guilding (2008) discovered that strategy has a positive impact on the implementation of strategic management accounting. Čater and Pučko (2010) found that SMEs do not have a clear plan and responsibility when deploying strategy. Their organizational strategy is very poor and features little commitment to the long-term development of the company. They need to be more expert at organizational strategy to enhance their role in the global network and work in integration with large companies (Bititci et al., 2012). Danneels (2002), Braam and Nijssen (2008) found that an organizational strategy with continuous product/services improvement, innovation and development promotes the adoption of the Balanced Scorecard in businesses.

Ownership

Ownership is considered a crucial factor in many business issues. Ownership can affect the decision to adopt or cancel a performance measurement system. Jensen and Meckling (1976) found that ownership determines the nature of a firm's business including business risk, the nature of real assets and cash, flow all of which influence the performance of a company. Mascarenhas (1989) suggested that ownership has two main components: (1) the benefits and limitations of the respective owner and of the respective managers, and the conflicts between owners and managers; (2) the capacities of these parties to affect resources and market factors (capital, management, technical factors). The different factors of the characteristics of ownership lead to different decisions about the development of the organizational resources, capacity, and strategy implementation. While some research argued that institutional constraints and organizational size are more important than ownership, Mascarenhas (1989) confirmed that the ownership approach provides a more developed theoretical basis for the explanation of an organization's strategy. Darnall and Edwards Jr (2006) found that the ownership structure impacts significantly on organizational strategy. While Kaplan (2001) and Niven (2008) supported that state-owned companies can adopt the Balanced Scorecard, Hoque (2014) confirmed that privately-owned and other sectors (joint-stock company, limited-liability company, etc.) implement the Balanced Scorecard as their preferable performance measurement system.

Structured on Contingency theory, the initial conceptual framework of this research comprises six contingent factors determining performance management systems: firm size, external environment, organizational culture, leadership, ownership, and organizational strategy. This present research tested the relevance of these contingent factors to the adoption of the Balanced Scorecard by Vietnamese SMEs. Figure 2.3 presents a diagram of the conceptual framework.

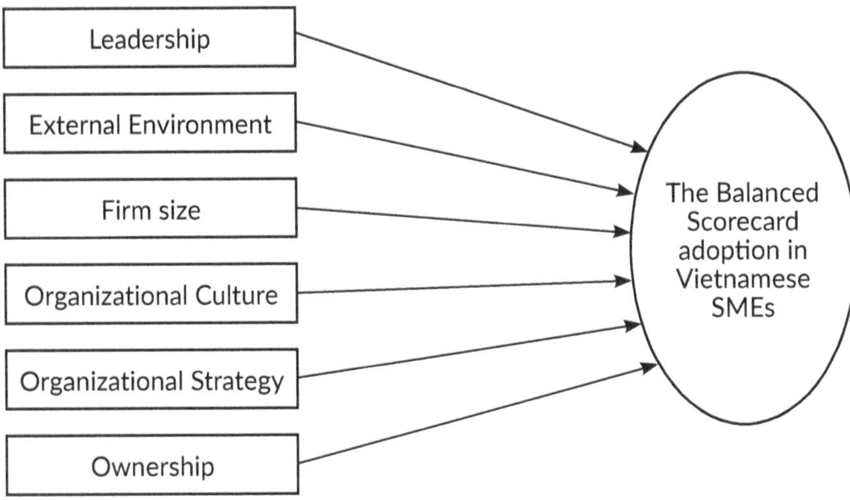

Figure 3.1 The initial conceptual framework

3.4. Conclusion

From its first introduction in 1992 by Kaplan and Norton to the present, the Balanced Scorecard has been adopted by different organizations, in different national and culture contexts (Hoque, 2014; Madsen, 2015). The Balanced Scorecard has been approved as a practical model and an important framework for performance management at the organizational level. However, most contextual research has been focused on Western and developed countries. Recently, the Balanced Scorecard has begun to be adopted in developing countries and in the SMEs context. As this adoption is recent, only limited research exists and more investigation is required.

The Balanced Scorecard has been an emerging issue in Vietnam over the last few years. Vietnam is a unique context with its emerging economy, dominated by SMEs. The adoption of the Balanced Scorecard by Vietnamese SMEs is under-researched. This chapter reviewed the theoretical and professional literature, which comprises mainly research from and about Western and developed countries. The chapter also discussed Contingency theory as the relevant theoretical basis for this present research. Six contingent factors are chosen as the initial templates for the investigation of the determinants affecting the adoption of the Balanced Scorecard in Vietnamese SMEs context. The methodology to conduct the research and the findings of research are presented and discussed in the following chapters.

Chapter 4

Why Have Vietnamese Small and Medium Sized Enterprises Adopted or Not the Balanced Scorecard?

4.1. Introduction

This chapter answers the first research question of "Why have Vietnamese small and medium sized enterprises adopted or not the Balanced Scorecard?" through a qualitative exploratory study. The six key themes that emerged from the literature review and were included in the interview guide were leadership, external environment, firm size, organizational culture, organizational strategy, and ownership. The semi-structured interviews were conducted with 32 participants who are top managers (executives), senior managers (heads of departments) and accountants from Vietnamese SMEs operating in various field and different provinces. Template analysis (King, 2004) was applied to analyze and search the transcripts for key themes. Given the specific features of the Vietnamese business environment, some valuable findings were made.

4.2. Sample description

Sample procedure

A total of 32 top managers (executives), senior managers (heads of departments) and accountants from SMEs operating in various fields (manufacturing, trading, and services), and in different provinces from the northern to the southern areas of Vietnam were included in the study. At this number of participants, the research reached the data saturation (Creswell, 1998, 2013; Ryan & Bernard, 2000; Saunders et al., 2017). The participants were sourced from the list of Master of

Business Administration (MBA) alumni and current MBA students of a Vietnamese University. An invitation email was sent to these people and followed up by phone calls to ask for their agreement to participate in an interview in a voluntary and confidential manner. The reason to focus on these people was that they were more likely to be involved in the decision about adopting the Balanced Scorecard in their company.

Participant demographics

Among the selected participants, there were 14 top managers, 10 senior managers and 8 accountants. The number of top managers is the greatest because they are the most significant people in all activities of their company. Based on their field of primary activity, 6 participants were working in the agriculture, forestry and fishery sector (4 top managers, and 2 senior managers), 10 participants in the industry and construction sector (3 top managers, 4 senior managers, and 3 accountants), and 16 participants in the trade and service sector (7 top managers, 4 senior managers, and 5 accountants). 25 participants were working in companies that had adopted the Balanced Scorecard (10 top managers, 8 senior managers, and 7 accountants), 7 people were working in companies that had not adopted the Balanced Scorecard (4 top managements, 2 senior managements and 1 accountant). The participants came from different parts of Vietnam: 14 participants (4 top managers, 6 senior managers, and 4 accountants) were from the South, 9 (5 top managers, 3 senior managers, and 1 accountants) in the Central part and 9 (5 top managers, 1 senior manager, and 3 accountants) were from the North.

Data collection

There were 32 individual face-to-face interviews conducted. Each was limited to a maximum of one-hour duration and based on a set of topic headings to guide the conversations. Consent forms and information sheets were provided in advance of the study. Participants were advised that information will be treated in the strictest confidence and none of the participants provided would be individually identifiable in the resulting book, report, or other publications. Theoretical saturation was achieved when we were unable to identify any new themes (Creswell, 1998, 2013; Ryan & Bernard, 2000; Saunders et al., 2017). Transcripts were sent to the participants for verification.

The interview protocol focused on two parts: (1) background information about the adoption/non-adoption of the Balanced Scorecard in the participant's company and (2) factors that impact on the decision to adopt/not adopt the Balanced Scorecard in the participant's company. Part 1 consisted of questions about the name of company, main activity field, the situation of Balanced Scorecard adoption (adopted or non-adopted, years of the Balanced Scorecard adoption, level of the Balanced Scorecard adoption (the whole company or some parts). Part 2 consisted of six impact factor-oriented questions based on the Contingency theory and other research in other countries. To enrich the content of the main questions, sub-questions were asked. The interview guide also included an open-ended question about other impact factors and how they affected the decision to adopt/not adopt the Balanced Scorecard in the participant's company.

Data analysis

The transcripts were analyzed and interpreted for key themes by using template analysis (King, 2004). Template analysis usually starts with some predefined themes intended to help guide analysis. These predefined themes were derived from the research literature. The data set was then analyzed using the predefined themes as a starting point to guide the development of the final template (Sidani & Al Ariss, 2014)

The initial template in this study started with two categories. The first category contained six general impact factors on the decision of Balanced Scorecard adoption. The second category was related to the Balanced Scorecard adoption in the Vietnamese context. From the interview responses, new themes emerged and provided additional information for the final template.

Initial template
Leadership
(Braam & Nijssen, 2008; Hambrick & Mason, 1984; Hendricks et al., 2004; Murphy & Southey, 2003)
Top management involvement
(Al-Omiri, 2003; Braam & Nijssen, 2008; Glaser et al., 2015; Volery et al., 2015)
Top management support
(Al-Omiri, 2003; Braam & Nijssen, 2008; Glaser et al., 2015; Volery et al., 2015)
Senior management involvement
(Bisbe & Barrubés, 2012; Chan, 2004; Inamdar et al., 2002)
External environment
(Chenhall, 2003; Kaplan & Bruns, 1987)
The intensity of market competition
(Abdel-Maksoud et al., 2005; Ahmad & Zabri, 2015; Chenhall & Morris, 1986; Luther & Longden, 2001; Mia & Clarke, 1999)
The support of local government
(Bertolini & Giovannetti, 2006; Meyer & Nguyen, 2005; Tran et al., 2009)
Firm size
(Ahmad & Zabri, 2015; Burns & Stalker, 1961; Chenhall, 2003; Fakhri, 2012; Hendricks et al., 2012; Hoque & James, 2000; Lawrence & Lorch, 1967; Liu et al., 2014; Oghuvwu & Omoye, 2016; Quesado et al., 2016; Speckbacher et al., 2003; Vo & Pham, 2018; Woodward, 1980)
Revenue
(Hoque & James, 2000)
Total assets
(Hoque & James, 2000)
Number of employees
(Hoque & James, 2000)
Organizational Culture
(Baird et al., 2004; Burns & Stalker, 1961; Chenhall, 2003; Chia & Koh, 2007; Henri, 2006; Kumar, 2001; Robbins, 2006)

Initial template
Outcome orientation organizational culture
(Kumar, 2001; Robbins, 2006)
Innovation organizational culture
(Kumar, 2001; Robbins, 2006)
Team orientation organizational culture
(Kumar, 2001; Robbins, 2006)
Attention to details organizational culture
(Kumar, 2001; Robbins, 2006)
Organizational Strategy
(Bititci et al., 2012; Čater & Pučko, 2010; Chenhall, 2003; Dinh et al., 2018; Fakhri, 2012; Garengo & Biazzo, 2012; Garengo & Bititci, 2007; Hendricks et al., 2012; Liu et al., 2014; Vo & Pham, 2018)
Continuous product/services improvement
(Braam & Nijssen, 2008; Danneels, 2002)
Innovation and development
(Braam & Nijssen, 2008; Danneels, 2002)
Ownership
(Darnall & Edwards Jr, 2006; Jensen & Meckling, 1976; Mascarenhas, 1989)
State-owned
(Kaplan, 2001; Niven, 2008)
Privately-owned
(Hoque, 2014)
Other sectors
(Hoque, 2014)

Table 4.1 *Initial template*

All interviews were coded, and quality checks and reflexivity methods were used to improve the reliability and validity of the coding process. We coded a sample of the data independently before cross-checking for similarities and differences to adjust the themes. We also asked the participants for feedback after completing the interview transcripts.

4.3. Findings and Discussion

This study found that a significant number of Vietnamese SMEs have adopted the Balanced Scorecard to manage their performance. However, the number of SMEs adopting the Balanced Scorecard is uneven in different parts of Vietnam. 25 out of 32 participants come from Balanced Scorecard adopter SMEs and most of them are from the southern provinces in Vietnam while most of the participants that come from Balanced Scorecard non-adopter SMEs are from the middle land of Vietnam.

Through the interviews and template analysis framework, the following findings helped addressing the question of why Vietnamese SMEs have adopted or not adopted the Balanced Scorecard.

Leadership

The first factor in focus in the literature review was leadership. Managers, especially top managers, generally have the most influential position in the decision-making process of an organization's strategy, design, and management system. It could be said that the organization is a reflection of its top managers (Braam & Nijssen, 2008; Hendricks et al., 2012; Tran, 2012).

Wang (2016) indicated that the structure of the Balanced Scorecard is designed from top to bottom. Strategy formulation is set up by top management and is then translated into a performance management index system that employees rely on to achieve the goals of a company. It is argued that leadership is involved in the whole process of Balanced Scorecard adoption and implementation.

Initial template: Leadership	Final template: Top management
Top management involvement	Top management qualifications and awareness
Top management support	Top management commitment
	Interdepartmental communication

Table 4.2 *Initial and final template of Leadership*

All participants identified the leadership as the most important reason for the decision to adopt the Balanced Scorecard in Vietnamese SMEs. Explicitly, they defined leadership as top management qualifications and awareness, and top management commitment.

Top management qualifications and awareness

According to the CEO of an agribusiness SME, qualifications and awareness of top management significantly affect the understanding, dissemination, and application of the Balanced Scorecard in an organization. She emphasized:

> The qualifications and awareness of top management determine the success and effectiveness of the adoption of the Balanced Scorecard. Top management needs to have a deep understanding of the Balanced Scorecard and its benefits, indicators, and standards. Then, they are confident in their decisions and participate effectively in the Balanced Scorecard adoption project. (CEOASA1)

A senior manager of an SME that has not adopted the Balanced Scorecard emphasized the role of the qualifications and awareness of top management in the decision to adopt or not adopt the Balanced Scorecard:

> Our director was not conscious of the Balanced Scorecard as a priority or had the major desire for any change. He did not realize this model can improve the business performance of the company in the future. (SMPCSN8)

The impact of the qualifications and awareness of top management on the decision to adopt the Balanced Scorecard in SMEs was also mentioned by an accountant of an SME that adopt the Balanced Scorecard:

> The qualifications and awareness of top management are extremely important. If the management does not understand deeply about the Balanced Scorecard, it leads to unbalanced and uncontrolled implementation, increasing the risk of issues related to capacity, influence, determination, etc. Top management needs to be aware that the Balanced Scorecard deployment takes time for effectiveness. They need to have a clear plan and define what the business will achieve and will not achieve in the short-term to avoid misunderstanding and frustration. (ACCHSA3)

To support the above comments, a director of a software SME that had adopted the Balanced Scorecard opined:

> Many directors of SMEs responded in a vague way when they were asked about the Balanced Scorecard, and its benefits as well as the plan to adopt the Balanced Scorecard in their businesses. Obviously, this will lead to a failure in the Balanced Scorecard deployment even though the Balanced Scorecard is a very effective performance measurement system. (CEOSNA9)

Top management commitment

All participants agreed that not only qualifications and awareness but also the commitment of top management are determinants of Balanced Scorecard adoption in Vietnamese SMEs. Top management commitment is a prerequisite for the successful adoption of the Balanced Scorecard. If the top leader of the SMEs does not end up with a model of change for the better, the application cannot succeed.

> Many Vietnamese SMEs were stopped from adopting the Balanced Scorecard because the top management were not committed to the end. (CEOCMA3)

> The adoption and implementation of the Balanced Scorecard involve all departments of enterprises. If the top management consider that this application is not directly related to their mission, they do not have commitment and strong direction, and then the project will be stuck. (SMHCNA6)

> It would be an inaccuracy if the business executives think that only the human resource department or the team can manage the Balanced Scorecard adoption. (SMHAMA3)

With full knowledge, awareness and commitment, top management will orient and lead their members to follow the goal of adopting the Balanced Scorecard. Top management will clarify the company's expectations for KPIs and targets, control the progress of the project and maintain project goals by continually promoting and encouraging staff during the process of building and operating the system. The commitment, consistency, feedback, and motivational measures of the top management for the whole company will solve the disagreements among parts of company that arise from the number of indicators, goals, KPI or measurement tools. They decide which systems will be connected to the Balanced Scorecard, such as the reward fund was based on the Balanced Scorecard score, and the promotion criteria were based on individual performance scores.

Interdepartmental communication

Most participants agreed with the influence of inter-departmental communication on the decision to adopt the Balanced Scorecard in SMEs. They considered inter-departmental communication as a network of information transmission. It links all units and departments in a company to transfer the information from top to bottom and vice versa. Lack of interdepartmental communication will lead to a low strategy awareness and Balanced Scorecard recognition for employees.

With experience of Balanced Scorecard adoption of around 6 years, the CEO of a software SME in the northern area of Vietnam said that:

> Our company faced many difficulties at the early time of Balanced Scorecard adoption because of the disagreement of members in the company. Most of them did not recognize how good the Balanced Scorecard is; they only thought that they have to work harder than before. However, our company has done very well with the interdepartmental communication. Explanation of the Balanced Scorecard is organized through annual internal conferences, adjusted to suit each stage of development. The method of communication is also flexible: depending on the subject, different situations have different explanations and approaches. Through this, all departments understand their role in the overall operation of company. After six years of Balanced Scorecard adoption, the interdepartmental communication always plays a crucial role in the implementation of the Balanced Scorecard and helps the company achieves more success. (CEOSNA9)

Another CEO of a company in the southern area of Vietnam that had adopted the Balanced Scorecard supported the relationship between interdepartmental communication and Balanced Scorecard adoption in SMEs:

> To adopt the Balanced Scorecard successfully, the management and staff of the company need to correctly understand the role of the Balanced Scorecard, the consistency of methodology, the way, and the actual implementation schedule. Through the interdepartmental communication, the information will be synchronized from the highest level to the employees. This helps the whole company to realize that the Balanced Scorecard is truly a tool for building, implementing, managing, and communicating the strategy across the organization. (CEOMSA13)

The Balanced Scorecard requires companies to have good interdepartmental communication so that information can be spread to employees in a timely fashion. In the process of the adoption and implementation of the Balanced Scorecard, without good inter-departmental communication, the information from top management to employees and the feedback from employees to top management will be stuck.

External environment

Initial Template: External environment	Final template: External environment
The intensity of market competition	The intensity of market competition
The support of local government	The support from business network
	Differences among the regions

Table 4.3 *Initial and final template of External environment*

The two key themes of external environment addressed are intensity of market competition and support of local government. The final template had the additional themes, arising from the interviews, of "the support from business networks" and "differences among the regions". The initial theme of "the support of local government" was not supported as significant in terms of the adoption of the Balanced Scorecard by the interviewees.

Intensity of market competition

All participants indicated that intensity of market competition is a key driving force behind the adoption of new management models, specifically the Balanced Scorecard. The participants emphasized the intensity of market competition in the sector that their companies are operating in as well as the number of competitors in the same sector which have adopted the Balanced Scorecard.

The participants confirmed the intense competitiveness of the sector they are operating in has a significant effect on the existence and growth of the business. This further motivates their companies to seek solutions to overcome competitive pressures and ensure sustainable development. For companies operating in an intensely competitive sector, applying the Balanced Scorecard for better progress is the best solution (CEOASA1, ACCSSA1, SMCFaMN2, ACCHSA3, SMHAMA3, ACCTNA4, CEOBNA5, SMHCNA6, CEOAMN10, ACCMNA6,

SMFBSA9, SMSHMA10, and ACCCNA8). The influence of the intense competitiveness in the operating sector on the decision to adopt the Balanced Scorecard was expressed by SMFBSA9 as follows:

> My company is operating in the banking and finance sector which is highly competitive. More banks and credit institutions are operating, which means we will face a lot of difficulties to retain old customers and attract potential ones. We discussed carefully to find a synchronous solution that can enhance the reputation of the business. As a result, we decided to adopt the Balanced Scorecard. We have used the Balanced Scorecard for five years and it has brought our company many benefits. The ability to manage the company is better; the number of customers is getting bigger and bigger; our prestige improved; we have been assessed as one of the best banks in many years. (CEOBNA5)

The intense competitiveness stimulates the companies to create a competitive advantage by differentiating itself from competitors. The interviewees confirmed that the Balanced Scorecard adoption is a good choice for this difference.

> The companies that operate in the same industry are interdependent, and the actions of one company often involve responses from the other ones. They are different in resources and abilities, but they have the same market; therefore, they always try to find ways to differentiate themselves from their competitors. Previously, there were only a few enterprises operating in seafood export business, and our company was extremely fortunate. However, competition pressure is getting worse as more and more businesses join in this field. We decided to change and renew our business. Seven years ago, we decided to apply the Balanced Scorecard to achieve better management performance. Since then, we have been able to create a competitive advantage for ourselves in an aggressively competitive environment. (CEOFSA4)

In addition to the intensely competitive pressure from the industry, the fact that competitors have been applying the Balanced Scorecard and other similar performance management models also has a great impact on the decision to apply the Balanced Scorecard of a business. Choosing to apply an effective management model can help the company creates sustainable differences in the market: a greater value for customers than competitors or comparable values at lower costs.

CEOCMA3, the director of a construction company located in the central region of Vietnam expressed his company's decision to adopt the Balanced Scorecard as follows:

> Our company has been operating in the market for nearly 20 years. In the field of our operation, there are more and more competitors. To gain a foothold in the market, businesses have been finding many ways to refresh and improve themselves. Around 2009, the Balanced Scorecard has become widely known as a very effective management model, especially in SMEs. Some of our rival businesses have begun to adopt this model and have achieved the desired results. From that, many enterprises operating in this sector have learned and we decided to apply this model. This has led us to explore this system carefully and decide to apply the Balanced Scorecard in 2013. (CEOCMA3)

Agreeing with CEOCMA3, CEOMSA13, the director of a manufacturing company located in the South of Vietnam also affirmed that a large number of competitors have applied the Balanced Scorecard and other similar models which encouraged his company to adopt this model. This model has general principles, and each enterprise has their own way to run this model to create their own values.

To deal with the market competition, most participants had a positive attitude toward adopting a new technology, products, and management practices to improve their ability to compete.

> SMEs need to apply the modern management system to use reasonably and maximize human and financial resources and

> harmonize the benefits and the conflicts between the members of the company. (CEOFMA8)

> Technology will help SMEs manage their business more efficiently, save costs and reach more customers. (CEOTeNA11)

Most of the participants argued that the intensity of market competition is the driving force behind the adoption of new management models, specifically the Balanced Scorecard, since that helps SMEs turn their strategy into actions quickly so that they can respond to challenges and exploit opportunities.

A chief executive of a software SME in the Northern area that had adopted the Balanced Scorecard over 5 years supported the importance of Balanced Scorecard adoption in businesses:

> In the seriously competitive environment, companies need to be stronger. The application of Balanced Scorecard helps businesses get balance, reduce vulnerabilities, and improve defense. It also helps businesses identify which stage of their growth should place emphasis on finance, customer, or learning. (CEOSNA9)

Sharing this viewpoint, a Human Resources manager of a Balanced Scorecard adopted SME that is operating in the telecommunication sector confirmed:

> The Balanced Scorecard adoption in SMEs is as a solution for sustainable development. It is a good tool to help SMEs solve problems, face risks, and develop feasible plans in the company. In the context of a highly competitive economy, it is necessary to set up a suitable strategic plan to deal with market fluctuation. (SMHTeSA1)

To confirm the driving force of the intensity of market competition behind the Balanced Scorecard adoption in SMEs, an accountant of a Balanced Scorecard adopted manufacturing SME presented his opinion:

> Applying the Balanced Scorecard to SMEs will help managers develop leadership strategies into specific management goals and action plans for each department and each employee. SMEs then will not worry about how to survive; they focus on building an internal force to develop and compete with other businesses. (ACCMSA2)

Support of local government

It has been argued that local government plays an important role in a business's performance, operation and development (Kokko & Tingvall, 2005; Nguyen et al., 2017). None of the participants from the interviews indicated that support from local government either through promotion of the Balanced Scorecard training, or financial support for its introduction, was an important driver of the adoption of Balanced Scorecard for their businesses. Indeed, some were quite critical on the role of local government in businesses, and of the reliability of the advice that local government provided.

Many participants supported the crucial role of local government in SMEs (but not in relation to the adoption of the Balanced Scorecard). They argued:

> Local government has an important influence on the development of operating SMEs in its management area. To survive and develop in an integrated economic environment, local government can help SMEs connect to the commercial supply chain. It also helps identify the strengths and weaknesses of SMEs and opens training programs to improve management skill of SMEs. Besides, local government can assist businesses in seeking external finance by providing partial credit guarantees, and extending collateral, as most SMEs find difficulty to access capital from banks. (CEOTSA2, ACCSSA1, CEOSMN6, SMFMSA5, SMFBSA9)

However, dealing with the Balanced Scorecard in Vietnamese SMEs, the support of local government is not considered an impact factor on the decision to adopt the Balanced Scorecard. An executive of a software SME, a human resources manager of a construction SME, and an accountant of a hotel expressed the same view about this issue:

> The support of local government plays an important role in the growth of SMEs, but the Balanced Scorecard adoption in SMEs is their own decision. To decide to adopt the Balanced Scorecard, SMEs need to consider both internal and external conditions. The support of local government is seen as a condition helping SMEs apply and run the Balanced Scorecard smoothly and effectively rather than a factor impacting the decision to adopt the Balanced Scorecard. (CEOSSNA9, SMHCNA6, ACCHSA3)

The support of local government does not affect the decision to apply the Balanced Scorecard as expected from the literature review. Instead, most of the participants confirmed that the decision to adopt the Balanced Scorecard at their company has been influenced by the support of business networks.

> In order to apply the Balanced Scorecard, we received great support from the business networks. The Small and Medium sized Enterprises Association at our company location has organized seminars and workshops to present and exchange both theories and practices of the Balanced Scorecard. (ACCMNA6)

> In the process of applying this model, we have received technical support and experiences from the enterprises that have successfully applied this model. Many businesses have been willing to advise and send their expert to help us. We also receive advice from external consultants. These help us to have a stronger determination to apply the Balanced Scorecard. (CEOTMA12)

Colclough et al. (2019) indicated that a business network is important because it provides explanation on the use of innovation strategies of SMEs. The findings of this study confirmed that the support of the business networks plays an important role in the decision of the Balanced Scorecard adoption in Vietnamese SMEs.

Evidence from the interviews also indicated that rather than the support of local government, the differences between the regions as a newly discovered element of the external environment influences the choice of Balanced Scorecard adoption in Vietnamese SMEs.

Differences among the regions

Before 1975, Vietnam was divided into two parts: the South of Vietnam was occupied by Americans, and the North of Vietnam belonged to the Democratic Republic of Vietnam. This led to differences in the socio-economic development between the two parts. While the South followed the capitalism style of the United State of America, the North applied a centralized economic model influenced by the Soviet Union. In 1975, Vietnam gained freedom. From 1975 to 1986, the country developed into a centrally planned economy and later shifted to a socialist-oriented market economy. However, due to historical circumstances, enterprises in different regions also have different operational characteristics.

Most of the participants confirmed that while SMEs from the Southern area are willing to adopt and implement new ideas quickly, Northern SMEs are conservative in making decisions, especially in applications of innovation. The interviewees also pointed out that SMEs in the Central region of Vietnam are divided into two groups: SMEs in South-Central region follow the style of Southern SMEs, and SMEs in North-Central region have similar characteristics to Northern SMEs.

These regional factors are also important to the adoption of the Balanced Scorecard. Most of the participating Southern SMEs had adopted the Balanced Scorecard for over 5 years, and the interviewees from these SMEs felt very excited about discussing the Balanced Scorecard topic. The SMEs from the Central and the North that adopted the Balanced Scorecard have a shorter time of adoption.

> Our company has implemented the Balanced Scorecard for 6 years. At that time, we were considered one of the SMEs pioneering in Balanced Scorecard adoption without any experience. However, with the desire to apply a useful management

> model as well as the great support from the consultants, we decided to adopt successfully. (CEOFSA4)

> In the era of globalization, the demand for information technology and modern management methods in enterprises are increasing. Taking opportunities and using timely appropriate management models will help businesses promote their strengths and overcome their weaknesses to achieve a stronger development. I realize that not only my business but also many SMEs around us are also approaching and adopting the Balanced Scorecard. By our own effort and the support of the business environment, the application of Balanced Scorecard in our enterprise took place smoothly and made some achievements. (ACCSSA1)

> We have known about that Balanced Scorecard and its benefits for a long time. However, it is not easy to make their decision to adopt this model for our company. Firstly, we do not want to change the current management model that we have used for a long time. Second, we feel awkward and unconfident to deal with many procedures and policies once we apply the new model. Third, the most important thing that we are waiting for is evidence of the success of Balanced Scorecard adoption in Vietnamese SMEs. (CEOHNN7)

It can be confirmed that Southern enterprises, including SMEs, are very active and self-motivated to adapt to change in the business environment. In addition, they rapidly access modern management tools to achieve better development. They are the driving forces for research and successful application of the Balanced Scorecard.

When we undertook the interviews with the representatives of SMEs in the Central region, we recognized the differences between SMEs from the South of Central region and SMEs from the North of Central region. Geographically, these SMEs are set up and operating in the Central region of Vietnam, but they are still affected by "business mechanism" of the North or the South. This was evident in the viewpoints of representatives of SMEs from the different areas of the Central region in Vietnam. A CEO from the Southern Central region of Vietnam said:

> In spite of our small business, we were looking forward to applying advanced management models for better growth. We were fascinated by the Balanced Scorecard, so we tried to investigate this model. We met consultants to ask about a successful Balanced Scorecard adoption. In addition, we received the willingness from many SME managers in our province and Southern provinces have successfully applied the Balanced Scorecard to share the Key Performance Index system to help us save time. (CEOTMA12)

A CEO from the North-Central region expressed a very different viewpoint:

> We are very cautious about applying the Balanced Scorecard or any new methodology in the enterprise. This has a significant impact on our operation, and expends our time, money, and human resources. Is it necessary to implement a new management model in a small size of company and market? (CEOAMN10)

Firm size

Initial template: Firm size	Final template: Firm size
Revenue	Human and financial resources
Total assets	Development stages of company
Number of employees	

Table 4.4 *Initial and final template of Firm size*

Much research literature has considered the size of a company as one of the main factors affecting the way an organization applies and uses management measures (Burns & Stalker, 1961; Chenhall, 2003; Hoque

& James, 2000; Liu et al., 2014; Oghuvwu & Omoye, 2016). Commonly, firm size is defined by its features relating to the number of employees, total assets, turnover, and budgets. However, in this study, the findings from the interviews pointed to organizational resources rather than firm size as influential on the decision to adopt or not adopt the Balanced Scorecard. Organizational resources here include human and finance resources, and the development stage of company.

Some participants stated that the size of a firm could affect the choice of Balanced Scorecard adoption in a SME. An accountant of a fashion business SME in the Southern area of Vietnam presented her view:

> At a small size of 20 employees and simple works, we prefer to apply a face-to-face management style rather than a modern performance management system. The Balanced Scorecard does not suit us. Using this modern system would costs our company more money and time. (ACCFaSN5)

Another interviewee, a CEO of a hotel in the Northern area of Vietnam stated:

> At present, our company is too small to concentrate on other perspectives outside the financial perspective. We do not think the Balanced Scorecard adoption is a good choice for us. (CEOHNN7)

An executive of a medium-sized fishery company in the Central area of Vietnam supposed:

> In SMEs, only medium-sized enterprises have enough conditions to apply the Balanced Scorecard to change and develop sustainably. (CEOFMA8)

On the other hand, most participants argued that firm size is not a key driving factor on the decision to adopt the Balanced Scorecard in SMEs in Vietnam.

An executive of a small company that adopted the Balanced Scorecard around 6 years ago expressed his opinion:

> Whatever size of enterprises in Vietnam, if they identify the importance of Balanced Scorecard, they can adopt the Balanced Scorecard to improve their performance management. Although they are SMEs, it is necessary to take up the Balanced Scorecard for long-term development with a larger amount of information, activity, strategy, and budget. (CEOTeNA11)

A finance manager of a manufacturing SME, who has played a crucial role in Balanced Scorecard adoption in her company confirmed:

> Size of company does not affect the adoption of Balanced Scorecard in SMEs. All SMEs, from micro to medium-sized can apply the Balanced Scorecard if the Board of Directors has strong determination. They are the leaders in the process of Balanced Scorecard adoption and implementation. (SMFMSA5)

From the explanations of the participants, the dimension of the business does not affect the decision to adopt the Balanced Scorecard in Vietnamese SMEs, however, the participants presented two factors related to organizational resources rather than firm size that could account for Vietnamese SMEs' decision to adopt or not to adopt the Balanced Scorecard. They are human and financial resources and the development stage of the SME.

Human and financial resources

Most of the participants indicated that limited human and financial resources prevent the adoption of new performance systems such as the Balanced Scorecard in SMEs. The adopting SMEs acknowledged that the adoption has been a costly process.

> SMEs generally do not have strong financial capacity and low effective management. This leads to increase management costs for the development of market and reduces the financial efficiency of enterprises. Thus, financial issues and expenses for the

> training, and technological investment are the big challenges for Vietnamese businesses. Costs also reduce the effectiveness of the Balanced Scorecard adoption and implementation in both large enterprises and SMEs. (CEO MSA13)

> The adoption and implementation of the Balanced Scorecard need businesses to invest the finance for consultant, training, implementing, etc. Some managers in some favorable conditions have developed the market very quickly, concentrating all market development resources on increasing sales in the short term but paying little attention to the development of management systems and financial resources for sustainable development. Therefore, enterprises often fall into financial difficulties (shortage of mobilize capital, investment capital). (SMFMSA5)

> Human resources also impact the adoption of the Balanced Scorecard. Staff must have knowledge to understand the role and benefits of the Balanced Scorecard. They need to follow the directives of company leaders and apply them to specific individual tasks. Balanced Scorecard adoption will not be successful if the staff does not have full understanding. (SMHCNA6)

In non-adopter SMEs, human and financial resources were considered as the reason why they have not adopted:

> The total number of staff is 20 persons of whom more than half are garment workers and salesmen. They are entirely submissive to superior orders. They have not proposed any new improvement for a better operation of the business. With the current limitation of human resource, it has not been able to adopt the Balanced Scorecard or any new modern management model in my company. (ACCFaSN5)

> We are not sure whether we will adopt the Balanced Scorecard in the future. At present, we allocate the financial priority to expand our business, develop the new market rather than apply the Balanced Scorecard or other performance management

> systems. Balanced Scorecard adoption and implementation cost a great deal while our capital is limited. (CEOSMN6)

Development stages of company

Many interviewees mentioned the development stages of company as a reason for the decision to adopt or not to adopt the Balanced Scorecard. The company will decide to adopt the Balanced Scorecard or not depending on the stage of company: start-up, growth, stability, etc.

We found that the Balanced Scorecard adopters are the SMEs in the growth or stability stage while the Balanced Scorecard non-adopters are mainly the start-up SMEs. To successfully apply the Balanced Scorecard, an enterprise needs to build up and evaluate plans and targets based on an analysis of the value chain accrued over a period. The start-up SMEs do not have much experience in developing targets and plans, they base their decisions primarily on individual viewpoints. Also, the Balanced Scorecard adoption requires time to establish a set of performance measures to assess achievability goals. Thus, start-up SMEs tend to spend time on other tasks and use existing assessments from other companies instead of adopting the Balanced Scorecard in their company.

> Our company has been established for over 20 years, developing steadily and is on the rise. Five years ago, we found it necessary to apply the Balanced Scorecard to serve the business's performance management more effectively. After 5 years of Balanced Scorecard adoption, we believe that we have involved the Balanced Scorecard in time. If we had applied this model earlier, we would not have been successful because of the lack of experience, and financial and human resources, etc. (CEOTSA2)

> In my opinion, I do not think the start-up companies, especially SMEs, focus on the Balanced Scorecard adoption as their primary consideration. Commonly, at the beginning, these companies focus their attentions on how to manage and expand the capital, market, and customer. (CEOCMA3)

> Our company was established 2 years ago. In the role of director, my main concern is the sustainable development of the company. I knew the Balanced Scorecard is a very useful management model and I have participated in many workshops, seminars, and training courses on applying the Balanced Scorecard model for SMEs. Although experts have advised that my business can apply this model right now, I do not think so. With a start-up like my company, it is not necessary to adopt the Balanced Scorecard because we are concentrating on the financial perspective than other perspectives. If we adopted this model now, we would not succeed because we do not have much management experiences or much capital and human resources. (CEOAMN10)

Organizational culture

Initial template: Organizational culture	Final template: Organizational culture
Outcome orientation organizational culture	Decentralization
Innovation organizational culture	Innovation
Team orientation organizational culture	Collaboration
Attention to details of organizational culture	Ready to take risks

Table 4.5 *Initial and final template of Organizational culture*

The role of organizational culture in the adoption of the Balanced Scorecard by SMEs was one of the themes emerging from the literature review. Organizational culture refers to all the cultural values created during the existence and development of a business, that become the values, concepts, practices, and traditions of the enterprise's operation. Organizational culture governs the emotions, mindset, and behavior of all the enterprise's members in the pursuit and fulfilment of the corporate goals. In today's Vietnamese enterprises, especially SMEs, organizational culture is gradually being formed. Due to its specific situation, each SME follows different types of organizational culture that affect the decision to adopt the Balanced Scorecard in its business.

Outcome orientation organizational culture and decentralization

Outcome orientation is a type of organizational culture that is about the organization completing its mission successfully with making every effort and with courage, and skills. Teams in this style always feature competent and planned thinking, high commitment, taking precautionary measures before acting, and learning from their own mistakes. This style emphasizes results, achievement, and action as the most important values.

The CEO of a transportation SME in the Central region of Vietnam that has adopted the Balanced Scorecard supported the role of outcome-oriented organizational culture in making the decision to adopt the Balanced Scorecard:

> Our company always work strategically and as planned. We keep to the goal to the end and flexibly implement various action solutions to accomplish the task assigned. Hence, we prefer to apply a performance measurement system relevant to our style and the Balanced Scorecard is a good choice. (CEOTMA12)

However, to successfully achieve outcomes, most of the participants emphasized the role of decentralization. They suggested that the organizational culture needs to ensure decentralization in management so that all decisions and results do not depend entirely on the top management. They argued that to adopt the Balanced Scorecard successfully, SMEs must build up an organizational culture in which everyone must have the initiative and creativity to promote his or her specific role within a broad enough scope.

Our company decides to apply the Balanced Scorecard model when we really needed a reasonable, specific hierarchy in the company to achieve the results as planned. Six years from the application of this model, the decentralized implementation in our company is very clear, and we have achieved many successes in business operations and management. (CEOFMA8)

Innovation organizational culture

Enterprises with an innovation organizational culture prefer to apply new modern practices, which is a platform to support the successful adoption of Balanced Scorecard by SMEs.

> It was easy to convince our business to adopt the Balanced Scorecard because our company always like to learn and apply innovation to get better development. We have implemented so many new things and gained a lot of success, so we believe that applying Balanced Scorecard is just as successful. (SMFMSA5)

A senior manager in a non-adopting SME spoke about the role of innovation culture in relation to the adoption of the Balanced Scorecard:

> An absence of innovation culture that promotes the introduction of new practices and procedures may be a potential reason for the non-adoption of the Balanced Scorecard in our enterprise. (SMPCSN8)

Team orientation organizational culture and collaboration

Team oriented organizational culture emphasizes collaboration among employees. Members of these companies have more positive relationships with their managers and workmates. With closer association, all members of the company can easily understand sources of problems and determine relevant actions for all of situations.

Team orientation supports SMEs deploying the Balanced Scorecard in groups. All members in groups collaborate and help each other in works. All decisions are made by the team rather than by manager only. (ACCCNA8)

Detail-oriented organizational culture and willingness to take risks

Participants indicated that a detail-oriented culture always emphasizes details and precision. It means that these organizations attend to the accuracy and detail of information produced by the Balanced Scorecard.

> In my opinion, once a company intends to adopt the Balanced Scorecard, they need to understand clearly all mission, values, strategy, and vision. Detail-oriented companies prepare these duties cautiously. Once these companies adopt the Balanced Scorecard, this model will help to transform the company's mission, values, strategy, and vision into performance objective and measure them exactly. I am sure that this type of organizational culture is relevant to Balanced Scorecard adoption. (SMHTeSA1)

However, an important concern that the participants emphasized is the willingness to take risks. They confirmed this willingness has a great impact on the determination to adopt the Balanced Scorecard. Willingness to take risks will help businesses prepare clear and specific plans to handle the bad situations that occur when the application of this model is not as favorable as originally envisaged.

> The application of innovations in enterprises will bring new improvements but can also bring risks of failure and cost. In my opinion, businesses that are willing to take risks are eager to apply balanced scorecards or other improvements with the expectation of better performance. They are not afraid of failure because of careful readiness to face risks. (CEOSNA9)

Organizational strategy

Initial template: Organizational strategy	Final template: Organizational strategy
Continuous product/service improvement	Continuous product/service improvement
Innovation and development	Innovation and development

Table 4.6 *Initial and final template of Organizational strategy*

Business strategy exerts a vital impact on the design, adoption, and diffusion of innovation processes (Chenhall, 2003; Fakhri, 2012; Garengo

& Bititci, 2007; Hendricks et al., 2012; Liu et al., 2014).

All participants argued that the Balanced Scorecard can be only applied to businesses with a clear business strategy and communication. The Balanced Scorecard is particularly suitable for SMEs and other kinds of companies that have the strategy of maintaining the old market and meeting the new market.

A finance manager of a Balanced Scorecard adopting SME strongly supported the role of strategy in the Balanced Scorecard adoption in SMEs:

> The Balanced Scorecard is a strategic planning and management system designed in mind to link the process of managing an organization's performance with the strategy. It does not make sense if a business deploys the Balanced Scorecard without a business strategy. (SMFCSA4)

Contributing to this viewpoint, a director of another Balanced Scorecard adopting SME indicated:

> The business strategy greatly influenced the adoption and application of the Balanced Scorecard in our company. With the business strategy, the company identified the specific goals and built the performance monitoring indicators. It also helped us to develop a strategic map, which is one of the critical steps in implementing the Balanced Scorecard. (CEOTMA12)

Specially, he explained about the role of strategy in the adoption of Balanced Scorecard in SMEs as follows:

> The selection of target and metrics of the Balanced Scorecard perspective represents the strategic priorities of the company. In the financial perspective, if the company chooses a growth strategy (sales), the important goal will be to expand the product line, service, and increase new application, customers, and new market. From the customer perspective, the business

> only determines the value map to measure if the business previously identified the target customer. Similarly, a business strategy must decide which core activity or capability is the driving force for creating a competitive advantage. Then, goals and targets in the internal perspective must focus on measuring the changes of performance created that core competence. With a clear business strategy, and goals and targets in the perspectives will ensure consistency and align the company's goals. (CEOTMA12)

Kim and Kang (2016) suggested that a company needs to establish a clear strategy with expected goals, outcomes, and specific responsibilities of each participant when deciding to adopt the Balanced Scorecard because the Balanced Scorecard design and implementation is based on the company's strategy and transfers it into four perspectives (Wang, 2016).

Ownership

Ownership has been found as a crucial factor that affects the decision to adopt or cancel a performance measurement system (Doan et al., 2011; Le & Harvie, 2010; Smith, 2010).

The three key ownership themes addressed in this study are the public sector, the private sector, and other sectors.

Initial template: Ownership	Final template: Ownership
State-owned	-----
Privately-owned	Privately-owned
Other sectors	Other sectors

Table 4.7 *Initial and final template of Ownership*

Public sector

All of the participants indicated that the public sector is not the type of ownership that encourages the adoption of the Balanced Scorecard.

This was confirmed by a senior manager in a state-owned SME in the Southern area of Vietnam that did not adopt a Balanced Scorecard:

> Our company is state-owned with a centrally managed style. The capital of our company is allocated annually by the state. Besides, we also get other preferential treatments from the state. All activities in our company need to obtain the agreement of the state. Normally, we follow the action plan from the state. We do not think the Balanced Scorecard is necessary in our company. (SMPCSN8)

A director of another state-owned SME that did not adopt the Balanced Scorecard expressed his opinion about the decision:

> The director of a state-owned company is also a wage earner. They have managed the company only over one or two periods of five years, and after that, another person will replace them in this position. When applying a modern performance practice in this company, for instance, the Balanced Scorecard, it needs the commitment of leader to the end of the project. However, because of the state-owned company mechanism as I mentioned, it is not easy to adopt the Balanced Scorecard effectively when this director starts this project, but they cannot keep connected with it to the end. (CEOAMN10)

Private sector and other sectors

Most of the interviewees have a positive view of private and other sector SMEs in relation to Balanced Scorecard adoption.

> Excepting the state-owned companies, other types of enterprises may apply the Balanced Scorecard because they are not centrally managed. They are easy to decentralize for the managers; they stimulate the creativity of employees and are willing to change to absorb the new. (CEOFSA4)
>
> These companies are not entitled to preferential treatment from

the state, so they need to change to survive in the fierce competitive environment. (SMFCSA4)

4.4. Summary of results

Using data collected from semi-structured interviews and analyzed by the template analysis method, this chapter examined factors affecting the decision of the Balanced Scorecard adoption/non-adoption in the Vietnamese SMEs context.

Strong arguments have been made in the literature on performance management broadly, and the Balanced Scorecard explicitly regarding the important influence that context can have on the adoption and operationalization of these activities in organizations (Ax & Bjørnenak, 2005; Kaplan & Norton, 1996; Mehralian et al., 2017; Neely, 2005; Sartor, 2019; Sorooshian et al., 2016; Voelker et al., 2001; Watts & McNair-Connolly, 2012). Specifically, there have been calls to focus on SMEs, as distinct from multinational enterprises (Andersen et al., 2001; Falle et al., 2016; Giannopoulos et al., 2013; Madsen, 2015; Malagueño et al., 2018), and on new country context (Chong et al., 2019; Jabeen & Behery, 2017; Kim & Rhee, 2012). Consistent with previous research (Ahmad & Zabri, 2015; Cardoso Vieira Machado, 2013; Chenhall, 2003; Fakhri, 2012; Garengo & Bititci, 2007; Hendricks et al., 2012; Hoque & James, 2000; Liu et al., 2014; Oghuvwu & Omoye, 2016; Quesado et al., 2014, 2016; Speckbacher et al., 2003), in this book, we used Contingency theory as the lens to explore the Balanced Scorecard adoption in SMEs in Vietnam.

Study 1 focused on factors that influenced the decision to adopt or not adopt the Balanced Scorecard approach in Vietnamese SMEs. The initial template of contingency factors used in Study 1 was developed from the literature review presented in Chapter 2 & 3. The initial template and revised template based on the findings from Study 1 are presented in Table 4.9 below. While there were a number of similarities that were found between the literature and the comments made by the managers interviewed, there were also a number of key differences as shown in 4.9 and discussed in subsequent paragraphs.

Contingency factors from literature review	Findings of Study 1
Leadership	**Top management**
(Braam & Nijssen, 2008; Hambrick & Mason, 1984; Hendricks et al., 2004; Murphy & Southey, 2003)	
Top management involvement	Top management qualifications and awareness
(Al-Omiri, 2003; Braam & Nijssen, 2008; Glaser et al., 2015; Volery et al., 2015)	
Top management support	
(Al-Omiri, 2003; Braam & Nijssen, 2008; Glaser et al., 2015; Volery et al., 2015)	Top management commitment
Senior management involvement	
(Bisbe & Barrubés, 2012; Chan, 2004; Inamdar et al., 2002)	Interdepartmental communication
External environment	**External environment**
(Chenhall, 2003; Kaplan & Bruns, 1987)	
The intensity of market competition	The intensity of market competition
(Abdel-Maksoud et al., 2005; Ahmad & Zabri, 2015; Chenhall & Morris, 1986; Luther & Longden, 2001; Mia & Clarke, 1999)	
The support of local government	The support of business networks
(Bertolini & Giovannetti, 2006; Meyer & Nguyen, 2005; Tran et al., 2009)	Differences among the regions
Firm size	**Organizational resources**
(Ahmad & Zabri, 2015; Burns & Stalker, 1961; Chenhall, 2003; Fakhri, 2012; Hendricks et al., 2012; Hoque & James, 2000; Lawrence & Lorch, 1967; Liu et al., 2014; Oghuvwu & Omoye, 2016; Quesado et al., 2016; Speckbacher et al., 2003; Vo & Pham, 2018; Woodward, 1980)	

Contingency factors from literature review	Findings of Study 1
Revenue (Hoque & James, 2000) ***Total assets*** (Hoque & James, 2000) ***Number of employees*** (Hoque & James, 2000)	Human and financial resources
	Development stages of company
Organizational Culture (Baird et al., 2004; Burns & Stalker, 1961; Chenhall, 2003; Chia & Koh, 2007; Henri, 2006; Kumar, 2001; Robbins, 2006)	**Organizational Culture**
Outcome orientation organizational culture (Kumar, 2001; Robbins, 2006)	Decentralization
Innovation organizational culture (Kumar, 2001; Robbins, 2006)	Innovation
Team orientation organizational culture (Kumar, 2001; Robbins, 2006)	Collaboration
Attention to details organizational culture (Kumar, 2001; Robbins, 2006)	Ready to take risk
Organizational Strategy (Bititci et al., 2012; Čater & Pučko, 2010; Chenhall, 2003; Dinh et al., 2018; Fakhri, 2012; Garengo & Biazzo, 2012; Garengo & Bititci, 2007; Hendricks et al., 2012; Liu et al., 2014; Vo & Pham, 2018)	**Organizational Strategy**
Continuous product/services improvement (Braam & Nijssen, 2008; Danneels, 2002)	Continuous product/service improvement
Innovation and development (Braam & Nijssen, 2008; Danneels, 2002)	Innovation and development

Contingency factors from literature review	Findings of Study 1
Ownership (Darnall & Edwards Jr, 2006; Jensen & Meckling, 1976; Mascarenhas, 1989)	**Ownership**
State-owned (Kaplan, 2001; Niven, 2008)	-
Privately-owned (Hoque, 2014)	Privately-owned
Other sectors (Hoque, 2014)	Other sectors

Table 4.8 *Study 1 Template*

The findings of Study 1 indicated that factors affecting the decision of to adopt or not adopt the Balanced Scorecard in Vietnamese SMEs context can be divided into three groups: external environmental factors, organizational factors, and leadership factors.

Firstly, the external environment was confirmed as the main factor impacting the decision to adopt the Balanced Scorecard in Vietnamese SMEs. The review of the literature suggests that the intensity of market competition and the support of local government are the external environmental factors that impact the decision to adopt the Balanced Scorecard by SMEs. However, this study found that, in Vietnamese SMEs, the intensity of market competition, the support of business networks, and differences among the regions are all related to the decision to adopt the Balanced Scorecard. SMEs that are operating in highly competitive sectors and SMEs with many competitors that have adopted the Balanced Scorecard tend to adopt the Balanced Scorecard more than other businesses. SMEs decide to apply the Balanced Scorecard in their company if they receive significant technical and advice support from the business networks and consultants. Because of historical circumstances, Southern and South-central SMEs in Vietnam are more willing to adopt the Balanced Scorecard than Northern and North-Central SMEs.

Secondly, the findings highlighted that resources, culture, strategy, and ownership are the main organizational factors influencing Vietnamese SMEs' decision to adopt the Balanced Scorecard. This study found that organizational resources rather than firm size affect the decision to adopt or not to adopt the Balanced Scorecard in Vietnamese SMEs. The SMEs with knowledgeable and skilled staff, stable financial resources, and in the growth or stability stage of development prefer to use the Balanced Scorecard to measure their performance. Moreover, the SMEs that feature decentralization, innovation, collaboration, readiness to take risks, and protection of their old market and readiness to develop new markets tend to apply the Balanced Scorecard. Additionally, the results of this study discovered that Vietnamese SMEs in private and other sectors are ready to apply the Balanced Scorecard and other similar performance measurement model to improve their performance while most state-owned SMEs do not consider about such models.

Finally, this study identified the importance of the Vietnamese SMEs leaders' decision to adopt the Balanced Scorecard. The literature mentioned both the roles of the top management and senior management in the adoption of a performance measurement system. The findings of this study focused especially on the qualifications, awareness, and commitment of top management and the inter-departmental communication of the company. In SMEs, top management directly manages the whole operation of company so the change must start from the top management. To successfully maintain the business in general and the Balanced Scorecard adoption in particular, top management must have relevant qualifications and awareness of their position, title, requirements, and assigned tasks. Thus, the commitment of top management is a prerequisite for the successful adoption of the Balanced Scorecard. In addition, businesses with a comprehensive interdepartmental communication system will ensure the information transfer clearly and motive the entire staff below.

4.5. Conclusion

There is little research on the Balanced Scorecard adoption in Vietnamese SMEs; therefore, this study (Study 1) is as an exploratory investigation of the factors that impact the decision of Vietnamese SMEs to adopt the Balanced Scorecard. In comparison with the initial factors identified from the literature review, the findings of this study (Study 1) discovered differences that contribute significantly to theory and practice and provided a better understanding of the adoption/non-adoption of the Balanced Scorecard by Vietnamese SMEs. They are (1) qualifications and commitment of top management rather than the involvement of both top management and senior management, (2) the support of business networks and regional differences rather than the support of local government, (3) organizational resources rather than the size of firm, (4) characteristics of organizational culture rather than the types, and (5) privately-owned and other types of ownership rather than all types of ownership including state-owned. These findings were used as a basis for Study 2 to explore how these factors affect the successful Balanced Scorecard adoption Vietnamese SMEs. Evidence from case studies of Study 2 is presented in the next chapter.

Chapter 5

How Do the Factors Influence the Successful Adoption of the Balanced Scorecard by Vietnamese Small and Medium Sized Enterprises?

5.1. Introduction

In Chapter 4, the answer to the first research question, "Why have Vietnamese small and medium sized enterprises adopted or not the Balanced Scorecard?" was reported as the results of Study 1 that involved 32 individual interviews and template analysis (King, 2004) was used to analyze and interpret the transcripts. Chapter 5 presents the evidence from case studies of four Vietnamese SMEs that had successfully adopted Balanced Scorecard to examine whether and how the impact factors found in the Study 1 affected their Balanced Scorecard adoption. The four SMEs were selected from the SME list of the Vietnam Prosperity Joint Stock Commercial Bank. Semi-structured interviews of individuals and focus groups, company documents, observation and bank assessments were used for collecting data. Template analysis (King, 2004) was applied to analyze data in three basic stages. The initial template of Study 2 was identified by the findings of Study 1.

Sampling procedures

The four successful Balanced Scorecard adopting SMEs were from the fields of manufacturing, agribusiness, software, and transportation. One SME is located in a Southern province of Vietnam, two in Central provinces (one in a North-Central province, and one in a South-Central province), and one in a Northern province of Vietnam. The SMEs were selected from the list provided by the Vietnam Prosperity Joint Stock Commercial Bank whose main customers are SMEs. According to Fernandes et al. (2006), the successful adoption of the Balanced Scorecard in SMEs can be recognized by their standard of quality control, their development and manufacturing plans, their methods of knowledge protection, their competing strategies, and product price policies. Successful adoption of the Balanced Scorecard also relies on improved cooperation among the different teams, a unified enterprise culture and the rapid response to market requirements.

Firstly, we contacted top managers of these four companies by mail and phone them to ask if they would like to participate in this study in a voluntary and confidential manner. We asked them to allow us to observe their processes of adoption and implementation of the Balanced Scorecard, give us access to their company's documents and staff involved in the Balanced Scorecard adoption, and finally, agree to being interviewed. Secondly, we contacted by mail and phone the staff involved in the adoption and implementation of the Balanced Scorecard that were introduced by the CEOs of these four companies to ask for their agreement to participate in this study in a voluntary and confidential manner, by completing an interview.

Table 5.1 summarizes the characteristics of the sample.

No.	Sector	Time of Balanced Scorecard adoption	Ownership type	Company location	Number of employees
Case 1	Manufacturing	7 years	Joint stock	North	98
Case 2	Software	4 years	Limited Liability	North-Central	50
Case 3	Agribusiness	3 years	Joint stock	South-Central	112
Case 4	Transportation	5 years	Joint stock	South	141

Table 5.1 *The profile of samples*

The following subsections outline the situation of the Balanced Scorecard adoption in each of the four companies.

Case 1: Balanced Scorecard adopter manufacturing company

Background of the company

This company is a joint stock company that has operated in the manufacturing sector for over 20 years. This company is located in the north of Vietnam and employs 98 persons.

Since 2011, this company has deployed a long-term business strategy using the strategic map model as well as adopting the Balanced Scorecard to manage the strategy implementation process. The application of the Balanced Scorecard over 7 years has helped the company to achieve its objectives: to evaluate its performance more comprehensively, to improve satisfaction of customers and employees, to manage and use capital and cost effectively, to link strategy of the whole company with employee activities, to incorporate each strategic target with resource allocation process, and to create a strong transition and greater flexibility for the company.

Description of the Balanced Scorecard adoption

The Balanced Scorecard adoption and implementation brought many good results in the operation and development of the company in the following four perspectives:

Financial perspective: Total annual revenue has grown significantly; the average annual growth rate is 15%. Profit target reflects the impressive and stable growth of the score on both gross profit and after-tax profit targets, meeting the company's expectation on applying the Balanced Scorecard. Operating costs tend to improve over time.

Customer perspective: This perspective meets the expectation of improving customer satisfaction level for the company when applying the Balanced Scorecard model through on-time delivery targets, increasing the successful transaction rate, becoming a strong brand name company, and increasing customer satisfaction.

Internal Business Process: This perspective is assessed on two main components, the level of internal process improvement, and strengthening and increasing labor productivity. The degree of completion of the internal process has been increasing year by year, indicating that the system of processes and personnel policies of the company has improved. The company has continued to invest in modern machinery and equipment for production of its strategic products. Initiatives and improvements on production lines and equipment have also been effective. Research products and market development are also attended to, so the indicators of "strengthening and increasing labor productivity" over the years have reached and exceeded the set targets. This result meets the goal of increasing employee satisfaction to the company, contributing to help the company stabilize resources, and building an attractive labor environment.

Learning and Growth perspective: This perspective is quite stable and tends to improve over time. It is applied to 100% of individuals and units, and all are included in the grading system according to KPIs. Training plans of each unit are fully identified and gathered into training plans for the entire company. The training programs take place according to plan and schedule, and the assessment clearly reflects the effectiveness of training. The indicators of this aspect are well implemented, contributing to meeting expectations: aligning the company's strategic objectives to each unit and individual, and comprehensive evaluation the labor performance of each individual and unit.

Case 2: Balanced Scorecard adopting software company

Background of the company

This company has operated for more than 10 years in this area and adopted the Balanced Scorecard 4 years ago. It is located in the North Central region of Vietnam. Operating in the high-tech area, the company understands the important role of the Balanced Scorecard in the business, especially in SMEs. Despite being considered a young company with less experience in doing business, and facing many difficulties, this company successfully applied the Balanced Scorecard to improve its development.

Description of the Balanced Scorecard adoption

Implementation results after 4 years of using the Balanced Scorecard always exceeded the planned targets in all four perspectives.

Financial perspective: Increasing turnovers in all the business activities of the company; increasing average turnover on each customer; decreasing the cost of turnover in all of business activities of the company; decreasing the cost on turnover in each business activity.

Customer perspective: Increasing customer satisfaction by reducing the percentage of returned goods on total sales; retaining customers through increasing revenue from existing customers; expanding markets, increasing new customers through increasing revenue from new customers on total revenue.

Internal Business Process: Improving production and business activities by ensuring the supply of high standard goods and services; the number of customers complaining about the quality of products and services is decreasing.

Learning and Growth perspective: The number of key leaders has been gradually reduced, the number of staff with knowledge and experience has increased. Employees' perceptions change positively when personal interests are associated with unit interests. Developing a mechanism of remuneration, reward, and reward policies to help balance resources appropriately, and improve employee productivity and income in a sustainable manner.

Case 3: Balanced Scorecard adopting agribusiness company

Background of the company

This is a fertilizer trading company with main products of micro organic fertilizer, foliar fertilizer, and fertilizer for perennial industrial plants, located in the South of Central Vietnam. This company is applying the Balanced Scorecard for the third year. Currently, the company is operating strongly in the domestic market for industrial crops such as rubber and coffee. It is also exporting to some Southeast Asian markets such as Laos and Cambodia.

Description of the Balanced Scorecard adoption

For more than 3 years, the company has successfully built and applied the Balanced Scorecard. This has helped the company identify its vision, mission, core values and build a sustainable development strategy, and support the transformation of the company's strategy and vision into specific objectives, measurements and clear targets by establishing an effective measurement system for job management. During the implementation process, the Balanced Scorecard also brought some general results for enterprises as follows:

Financial perspective: Raising equity and reduce liabilities on revenue; reducing fixed costs over the years: 2018 was 27.25% compared to 33% in 2015; increasing gross profit margin over the years: 2018 was 39.41% compared to 31% in 2015; increasing sales in the period: 2018 reached 8.75% compared to 5.2% in 2015.

Customer perspective: Increasing distribution network to meet customers' requirements.

Internal Business Process: Impacted on employees' awareness of the importance of evaluating the efficiency of processes, instead of just working on that process, thereby improving internal assessment skills for employees through the training and practical training sessions. Supported management to effectively manage the entire system of the company. Based on the performance of the whole system, management will decide new strategies / adjust financial processes and business production to suit the development of the company.

Learning and Growth perspective: Improved teamwork and accountability of departments / individuals through dividing work groups into four perspectives: Financial, Customer, Internal Business Process, Learning and Growth. Created cohesion among departments in the process of applying the Balanced Scorecard and created a habit of statistics, drawing graphs to track KPIs and making monthly reports, analyzing causes, and finding solutions to overcome targets not achieved.

Case 4: Balanced Scorecard adopting transportation company

Background of the company

This company is located in the South of Vietnam. It adopted the Balanced Scorecard 5 years ago. This company has been considered a fast developer with a high rate of market expansion; its operation efficiency has increased year after year. However, this company has many problems in business operations and strategic implementation. Finding a powerful tool to be able to effectively implement business strategies and assess business operation more fully and reliably is necessary. The Balanced Scorecard is a relevant choice of the company.

Description of the Balanced Scorecard adoption

After five years adopting the Balanced Scorecard, the company has achieved certain successes in all four perspectives.

Financial perspective: The revenue and profit of the company has tended to increase; the total capital of the company also has increased over the years, showing that the financial perspective of the company is effective. Considering the current economic context, the company's efforts are notable. The average labor productivity per employee also increased, showing that in the financial aspect, the company also uses more efficient labor resources, which contributes to increase the business performance of the company. Profit rates have tended to increase, indicating that the efficiency of business capital use has also tended to rise, reflecting the positive situation in the business operations of the company. In addition to paying attention to financial results, the company also considers the relationship between profit and cost, in order to use economically and efficiently resources.

Customer perspective: Recently, the company has signed many great value contracts with customers. The company has close customers signing many contracts, which reflects the trust of partners with the company. When the company satisfies customers, it leads to long term cohesion between customers and company. The survey showed that customers are also satisfied with the company about products, employees, convenience of distribution channels or flexibility in payment. This reflects the success of the company in establishing relationships with customers.

Internal Business Process: In this perspective, the company has focused on customer information, smart storage, and customer needs, and focused better on recording and following the characteristics of each customer. Research activities on competitors are also implemented quite carefully to promote the advantages of products. Advertising and management activities are paid attention to by the company. The company started to build indicators to manage the operational processes of each department and individual.

Learning and Growth perspective: Thanks to certain attention and reward, the recruitment mechanism is transparent, open, and the cohesion of the staff is tight, dynamic, and enthusiastic. The company has been interested in qualified training to improve the skills needed for employees in advertising, marketing, market exploitation. The company is active in building goals and measures in training and development factors associated with the company's development strategy. In particular, the company also developed criteria to assess the perspective of Learning and Growth according to the Balanced Scorecard.

Participant demographics

There were 15 interviewees coming from 4 successful Balanced Scorecard adopting companies, those that were the subject of the case studies. These participants were chosen by the introduction of the CEOs of these companies because they were more likely to be involved in the decision to adopt the Balanced Scorecard in their companies. Four interviewees came from a manufacturing company, four come from a software company, three were in an agribusiness company, and four were in a transportation company. The interviewees have over 5 years of working experience and qualifications of Bachelor or Master's degrees. All interviewees have a deep understanding of the Balanced Scorecard adoption and implementation in their companies because they were related to this process from the beginning of application. Table 5.2 presents the profile of the interviewees.

Co.	Position	Time of working in the company	Qualifications	Interview code
Manufacturing	Director	20 years	Master of Business Administration	CEO1
	Finance manager	13 years	Bachelor of Accounting	FM1
	Human resource manager	9 years	Bachelor of Business Management	HRM1
	Information technology manager	5 years	Master of IT	ITM1
Software	Director	10 years	Master of Business Administration	CEO2
	Finance manager	7 years	Master of accounting	FM2
	Human resource manager	10 years	Bachelor of Business Management	HRM2
	Information technology manager	5 years	Master of IT	ITM2
Agribusiness	Director	11 years	Master of Business Administration	CEO3
	Financial manager	7 years	Master of Accounting	FM3
	Business development manager	10 years	Master of Business Administration	BDM3
Transportation	Director	10 years	Master of Business Administration	CEO4
	Human resource manager	10 years	Bachelor of public Administration	HRM4
	Business development manager	6 years	Master of Business Administration	BDM4
	Car operating manager	8 years	Master of Business Administration	COM4

Table 5.2 *Profile of interviewees in the four case studies*

Data collection

For data collection, we used semi-structure interviews and documentary analysis. Documentary analysis was used primarily to provide the evidence for the successful adoption of the Balanced Scorecard in these case studies. By analyzing financial statements, bank statements, tax reports, and other related documents, we explored the background information about these companies' experience of the Balanced Scorecard.

Two focus group interviews with the participants involved in the adoption of the Balanced Scorecard from manufacturing company (case 1) and transportation company (case 4), and seven individual face-to-face interviews with Director, Finance manager, Human Resource manager, Business Development manager and Information Technology manager from the software company (case 2) and the agribusiness company (case 3) were conducted. Case 1 and case 4 preferred to take part in focus group interviews because they had weekly meeting to discuss the Balanced Scorecard adoption in their company. They allowed us to conduct the focus interviews at the same time of the meeting to save time. In addition, the participants believed that participating in focus group can help the conversations develop naturally, the interaction of information between them can help to provide more detailed information. Other participants in case 2 and case 3 chose to take part in individual interviews because they can actively select the appropriate time and answer the interview freely without being influenced by the opinions and views of other participants. Each was limited to a maximum of one-hour duration and based on a set of topic headings to guide the conversations. The interview guide was used in differential and flexible ways, according to participants' position to encourage them to lead the discussion. Research consent forms and information sheets were provided in advance of the study. All information provided has been treated in the strictest confidence and none of the participants has been individually identifiable in the resulting book, report, or other publications. Transcripts were presented to each respondent for verification.

The interview protocol focused on the circumstances of the adoption of the Balanced Scorecard, the impact factors, and the way they affected the process of implementation of the Balanced Scorecard in the investigated case studies. The interviews involved six impact factor-oriented questions based on the findings of Study 1. They related to top management, external environment, organizational culture, organizational strategy, organizational resources, and ownership. Sub-questions and open-ended questions sought to elicit deeper and more detailed responses.

Data analysis

The transcripts of the semi-structured interviews were analyzed and interpreted for key themes by using Template analysis (King, 2004). Template analysis usually starts with some predefined codes intended to help guide analysis. These predefined codes were derived from the results of the Study 1 and underpinned by Contingency theory. The analysis data set then produced the final template consisting of the specific themes of this study.

The initial template in this study (Study 2) started with two categories. The first category included six factors drawn from the finding of Study 1 that impact the adoption of the Balanced Scorecard in Vietnamese SMEs. The second category consists of the sub themes of the main templates in the first category. Through the set of questions and response, new themes emerged and contributed to the final template.

All interviews were coded, and quality checks and reflexivity methods were used to improve the reliability and validity of the coding process. Firstly, we coded a sample of data independently and argued the similarities and differences to adjust the themes. After completing the interview transcripts, respondent feedback was sought. In addition, we reviewed carefully how assumptions about the phenomenon might impact the research question and the highlighted issues in the interview topic guide. Table 5.3 contains a priori themes taken from the results of Study 1 in chapter 4

Initial template
Top management
Top management qualifications and awareness
Top management commitment
Interdepartmental communication
External environment
The intensity of market competition
The support from business networks
Differences among regions
Organizational resources
Human and financial resources
Development stages of company
Organizational Culture
Decentralization
Innovation
Collaboration
Ready to take risks
Organizational Strategy
Continuous product/ service improvement
Innovation and development
Ownership
Privately-owned
Other sectors

Table 5.3 *Initial template*

5.2. Findings and Discussion

We conducted two focus group interviews with the participants from the manufacturing company (case 1) and the transportation company (case 4), and seven individual interviews with Director, Finance manager, Human Resource manager, Business Development manager and Information Technology manager from the software company (case 2) and the agribusiness company (case 3). The template analysis framework produced the following findings addressing the question of how the factors influence the successful adoption of the Balanced Scorecard by Vietnamese SMEs.

Top management

All the participants from the four case studies strongly supported the view that the CEO of SMEs is the most important person to impact both the decision to adopt the Balanced Scorecard in their company and the successful application of this model.

> In our company, the CEO was the first person to recognize the need to innovate for the better development of the company. He had to directly research and learn to make decisions for deployment throughout the enterprise. Once he decided to deploy, he had to commit to the end of project. (HRM1)

> In the situation of the company facing great competitive pressure, the CEO tried to find out an effective performance measurement model for the company to get a sustainable development. He was the first person to take part in the Balanced Scorecard training courses. He also invited consultants to facilitate the application of the Balanced Scorecard for company. Even now, when the Balanced Scorecard adoption has become successful, the director still takes part in the Balanced Scorecard process. (HRM4)

Initial template: Top management	Final template: CEO
Top management qualifications and awareness	Qualifications, awareness of CEO
Top management commitment	Commitment of CEO
Interdepartmental communication	Interdepartmental communication

Table 5.4 *Initial and final template of Top management*

Commitment, qualifications, and awareness of top management

It can be concluded that the commitment, qualifications, and awareness of the CEOs contribute to the successful adoption of the Balanced Scorecard. The CEOs recognize that it is necessary to apply an innovation such as the Balanced Scorecard to help the business define specific activities, consistent with the strategic objectives. They also remain deeply involved until the end of the adoption process to make sure the deployment works well. The strength of the Balanced Scorecard is maximized when it reaches a consensus with the CEOs of all members of the enterprise, aligning the goals of the organization with the goals of each individual in the organization.

> Realizing that the application of the Balanced Scorecard is reasonable and brings many benefits for businesses, I decided to learn and implement this method in my business. Initial implementation has encountered many difficulties, and sometimes I felt discouraged and ready to give up. I had to resolve to implement, create a favorable environment with well-prepared resources and make adjustments in time to successfully build a Balanced Scorecard for my company. (CEO2)

> At the beginning stage of the Balanced Scorecard adoption process, the management board of the company participated in consultancy courses on the Balanced Scorecard and methods of developing strategies and evaluating performance according to the Balanced Scorecard model. After taking the consultancy courses, the Director agreed to undertakings, commitments, and roadmap for implementation. (CEO1)

> Facing the need to expand the business market as well as to grow the company, I realized that the company needs to develop a more effective method of evaluating performance to overcome the limitations of our method of evaluating achievements in the present. Accordingly, the use of the Balanced Scorecard can help the company to evaluate its performance more effectively. The Balanced Scorecard provides a mechanism to control, eval-

> uate and fully exploit the key driving factors for the success of businesses. (CEO3)

> Deploying the application of the Balanced Scorecard to the company is the responsibility of top management and a prerequisite for success. From the analysis of factors such as the business environment, market development trend ... business leaders began to develop the overall development strategy for businesses. Then, based on the planned development strategy, businesses identify goals for four perspectives of the Balanced Scorecard. When the objectives are determined and approved, it is widely disseminated to each employee in the enterprise. (FM3)

The CEO's commitment and determination to persevere to the end is a prerequisite for the successful implementation of the Balanced Scorecard. Many businesses in Vietnam, both large companies and SMEs, have abandoned their Balanced Scorecard project because of the lack of director's determination.

> The CEO's commitment and determination to the end convinced all employees of the company to participate. Once they participate in the implementation, the project can be successful, and brings benefits to company and employees. Thereafter, they are more actively involved to make the project more and more successful. (FM2)

> We have the advantage of being a software business so many employees are good at technology. The Balanced Scorecard is a modern management method, involving a lot of Information Technology. However, it will be a mistake if only the project team will implement the Balanced Scorecard. We have technological knowledge, but we need the direction, supervision, and participation of CEO in every stage from deployment to implementation. (ITM2)

Applying new management tools and changing the traditional management way in the company is very difficult. Therefore, to have a Balanced Scorecard system operating effectively, first, leaders of the company must disseminate and implement changes in the company. The process of deploying the Balanced Scorecard system requires the active and regular participation of the CEO, which requires the CEO's knowledge and expertise.

> When deciding to apply the Balanced Scorecard in our business, I must regularly attend Balanced Scorecard-related training courses to improve my understanding, update my knowledge, and find out how to adopt and organize this model most effectively. (CEO4)

> The CEO's qualifications and awareness are very important in running the business activities, especially in the management of the application of an innovation such as the Balanced Scorecard. (HRM1)

Inter-departmental communication

The close association among the members of the company is very important in the application of any innovation. Good inter-departmental communication will ensure the information is shared among the different groups in the company and create a close relationship among these groups. Study 1 found inter-departmental communication as a top management factor impacting the decision to adopt the Balanced Scorecard in SMEs. Good inter-departmental communication will help the top management to strengthen their role in directing, monitoring, and supervising the process of Balanced Scorecard adoption. Study 2 confirmed the finding of Study 1 that interdepartmental communication influences the successful adoption of the Balanced Scorecard in Vietnamese SMEs.

> It is necessary to have a close relationship between departments and staffs in the company. It helps to build solidarity in dealing with collective affairs. The information will be clearly communicated across different levels thanks to good interdepartmental communication. When applying the Balanced Scorecard, we found that a close connection among departments of our

> company would greatly help the process of the smooth implementation of the Balanced Scorecard and information would be communicated promptly and exactly from the steering to the receiver. (ITM2)

> Once your company adopts the Balanced Scorecard or other innovation approaches, communication among employees helps to ensure the process of adoption runs seamlessly. Building an effective interdepartmental communication help to avoid confusion that normally happens in the process of information acquisition, transmission, and processing among departments of the company. When we first applied the Balanced Scorecard, we encountered many difficulties and confusion in developing and implementing the goals of financial and non-financial perspectives. However, the problems were soon solved thanks to the close association among the members of the company. (CEO1)

> Interdepartmental communication helps me a lot in the process of conveying my orders to the levels of the company, even directly to each employee and receiving feedback from them. The process of applying the Balanced Scorecard in the company primarily requires my responsibility. Without the close cooperation among departments, I would lack the support of staff in my management activities. (CEO4)

External environment

While the CEO is considered the very important internal factor affecting the decision of the adoption and successful application of the Balanced Scorecard in SMEs, the external environment is confirmed by all interviewees as a significant determinant motiv ating SMEs to select the Balanced Scorecard for better development.

The interviewees all agreed that the intensity of market competition, the support of business networks, and differences among regions are the external environment factors impacting the successful application of the Balanced Scorecard in Vietnamese SMEs.

Initial template: External environment	Final template: External environment
The intensity of market competition	The intensity of market competition
The support of business network	The support of business network
Differences among regions	Differences between the Northern and the Southern regions

Table 5.5 *Initial and final template of External environment*

The intensity of market competition

The intensity of market competition has emerged to be the most important external factor impacting the adoption of the Balanced Scorecard in SMEs.

> As a SME, to be able to compete, expand market share, retain old customers, and attract more new customers, we must focus on innovation and creativity in business methods and management models. The application of the Balanced Scorecard has helped us to create competitive advantages and sustainable development. (CEO3)

> We face a lot of strong competitors. They have also been applying many effective management models. This has motivated us to apply a modern management model in accordance with the present conditions of our business to help us grow sustainably. (BDM3)

These opinions came from the representative of the agribusiness. Agribusiness is a popular and competitive sector in the Central province of Vietnam because the main livelihoods of most local people are based on agriculture. Many companies in this sector have operated for a long time; however, the operation of the agribusiness SME in this case was not long enough to get a strong position in this sector. To compete with other companies, it was necessary to adopt a modern management approach. From the viewpoints of respondents, the intensity of market competition was really a strong determinant in the successful adoption of the Balanced Scorecard in their company.

The CEO and Business Development Manager of the transportation SME from the Southern province of Vietnam also stressed the impact of the intensity of market competition on the decision to adopt the Balanced Scorecard in SMEs.

> Our company has been operating in this sector for over 10 years. Previously, only a small number of companies operated in this field, therefore, competitiveness was not a problem. In recent years, the number of companies participating in this area has increased dramatically, which has led to the competitiveness becomes fierce. This forces us to adopt a modern management tool to improve the business performance. (CEO4)

> As a small-scale enterprise and operating in a fiercely competitive market, we need to manage the performance effectively. The Balanced Scorecard is a suitable choice. (BDM4)

The support of business networks

While the intensity of market competition has a major impact on the decision to adopt the Balanced Scorecard, the support of business networks affects both the decision to adopt and the successful application of this model for SMEs.

> Our company's achievements in the application of the Balanced Scorecard have greatly benefited from the help of the business networks. They advise us on the need to apply the Balanced Scorecard to improve the performance management. They help us to solve problems in the process of applying this model with their practical experiences they have accumulated during the application of the Balanced Scorecard in their companies. Thanks to the support of the business networks, we shortened the time and saved the organizational resources for applying model. (CEO2)

> The Association of Small and Medium sized Enterprises in our province regularly organizes workshops, seminars to exchange

> experiences on modern management models. Experts are invited to present academic knowledge and practical experience in the application of the Balanced Scorecard. These give us a deeper understanding and awareness of the need to apply the Balanced Scorecard model. (ITM1)

The support of the business networks in the application of the Balanced Scorecard will help SMEs save a lot of human and financial resources and shorten the investment time to achieve success in business management. Instead of having to learn new models and application procedures by themselves, SMEs receive a lot of support from the community. In this way, SMEs also avoid the failures that the previous enterprises have encountered and design for themselves a reasonable plan to adopt the Balanced Scorecard.

Differences among the regions

Study 1 found that differences among regions, the Southern provinces, Northern provinces, South-Central provinces, and North-Central provinces impact the decision to adopt the Balanced Scorecard in Vietnamese SMEs. However, the focus group and individual interviews of Study 2 showed that the successful adoption of the Balanced Scorecard in SMEs in Vietnam is affected by the differences between Northern region and Southern region, the Central region not exhibiting any differences from their neighboring Southern or Northern region.

> With more than twenty-years of doing business, I realize that enterprises in the Southern regions are very interested in the rapid growth. They are always looking for strategies and methodologies to develop their business, dominate the market, especially in fierce competition. We are one of these companies. We are willing to apply innovations in our business for more benefits. The Balanced Scorecard adoption is a good choice for this situation. (CEO2)

Many companies in the Southern regions like to seek and apply innovations to create a rapid and stable development. Similarly, businesses in the South-Central provinces take similar approaches. They are willing to adopt new performance management models to create a better future development. This was confirmed by the representative of the agribusiness SME in a South-Central province.

> Although there are differences in location, we have similarities in the way of building, operating, and developing business to SMEs in the Southern regions. We prefer to implement modern management models for a strong growth. Recognizing the superiority of the Balanced Scorecard and its applicability in SMEs, we decided to quickly adopt this model and achieved certain successes. (CEO3)

While the Southern and South-Central enterprises are willing to apply the Balanced Scorecard for a rapid development of their business, the Northern and North-Central companies are very cautious about applying modern management models. They are more concerned about safety and basic security needs are prioritized (Benzing et al., 2005).

> We had a hard time for building a business because of the disadvantages in the natural and socio-economic conditions. Therefore, we want to ensure the safety and sustainability of our business. The application of innovation can bring successes but can also bring great risks. We only decide to apply a new modern approach once we believe its feasibility. This proves that not many companies and SMEs in Northern region have applied the Balanced Scorecard or other management models. (CEO1)

> Although we operate in different regions, the northern SMEs and our company have the same business management style due to the impact of the State's economic management mechanism according to the central planned economy. Safety in business is the top requirement of our company. As an enterprise operating in the field of high technology, we readily recognize the superiority of modern performance management methods. However, to accept the application of these models, we need time to test the security that the models can bring to the busi-

> ness. We only decide to apply the Balanced Scorecard or other performance measurement management tool once we realized they could bring safety for our company. (CEO4)

It is evident that regional differences impact the success of the adoption of the Balanced Scorecard in Vietnamese SMEs through the values that the Balanced Scorecard brings to them. The Southern and South-Central SMEs that the mainly concentrate on rapid growth will be interested in adopting the Balanced Scorecard successfully to achieve better development. The northern and north-central SMEs motivated by the desire to ensure safety in business development will try to successfully apply the Balanced Scorecard for a sustainable growth.

Organizational resources

This study has consistently confirmed the results of Study 1 that human and financial resources and the development stages of a company are the organizational resources factors impacting the successful adoption and implementation of the Balanced Scorecard in Vietnamese SMEs. Regardless of firm size, a company with good preparation of resources can successfully apply and implement the Balanced Scorecard model. In addition, the development stage of the company also contributes to the likelihood of the success or failure of the adoption of the Balanced Scorecard in SMEs. A company in the stable development stage needs to apply the Balanced Scorecard for a sustainable growth rather than a start-up company.

Initial template: Organizational resources	Final template: Organizational resources
Human and financial resources	Human and financial resources
Development stages of company	Development stages of company

Table 5.6 *Initial and final template of Organizational resources*

Human and financial resources

All of participants from the four case studies confirmed the importance of human and financial resources to the successful adoption of the Balanced Scorecard in Vietnamese SMEs. They were aware the implementation of the Balanced Scorecard is a long process that requires careful preparation of financial and human resources.

> More than three years ago, when we decided to apply the Balanced Scorecard to our business, we prepared our financial and human resources very well. We understand that the application of innovation will be difficult, especially in small-scale enterprises, without careful preparation of these resources. The capacity of the director to apply the Balanced Scorecard is enhanced regularly through short-term training courses. The management team is equipped with analytical and problem-solving skills in the assigned areas. All employees are entitled to participate in Balanced Scorecard training courses to practice the assigned tasks in the best way. Besides, we have cut down unnecessary expenses to focus financial resources on Balanced Scorecard. (FM3)

> In our company, we had the training courses of the Balanced Scorecard for the whole company, from the top managers to the heads of departments and all employees. All staff of the company need to understand what the Balanced Scorecard is, how it works and the duty of each member of the company in this process. The company also holds the intensive training on the Balanced Scorecard for strategic management staff; asks the employees to actively learn, and participate fully in the Balanced Scorecard training courses, and contribute to adjust KPIs, solutions and initiatives to achieve better targets and objectives. They are also required to strictly implement the activities in accordance with the approved process. Additional, to successfully adopt the Balanced Scorecard, we prepared a clear, long-term financial plan. We know many cases of the Balanced Scorecard adoption having to stop in the middle because of lack of capital. We do not want to be like them. Although we need capital for investment in production expansion, the application of the Balanced Scorecard will help us develop sustainably. Investing in this project is necessary. (CEO1)

Once it is decided to implement the Balanced Scorecard or other kinds of innovation, the company's management committee and staff need to have relevant knowledge and experience in the field of innovation. They must take training courses frequently to update their knowledge and information. Not only human resources, but finance resources are also a big motivation for the company to adopt the innovation.

> The Balanced Scorecard refers to a series of key strategic solutions that are closely connected to objectives, helping to gradually achieve the strategic vision of the company. The main activities in the production and business at the company are usually undertaken by the central management such as heads and deputy heads of the departments, with the support of the overall coordination of the strategy and transformation committee led by the management board. In addition, the company's employees are also important persons who directly perform specific tasks. To help deploy the Balanced Scorecard successfully, project execution capacity, situation solving skills, discipline and flexibly in implementation methods, and mobilization skills are the key requirement of the management team. Besides, the company's employees need to have basic knowledge about the Balanced Scorecard. (HRM4)
>
> To adopt the Balanced Scorecard successfully, the company needs to invest in information technology, such as internal information system, customer data, and management software. The company needs to invest in infrastructure, and pay consultants, or invite experts to work with the company in this field of adoption. These activities take a large amount of money of our company; however, they bring many benefits to us as well. (BDM4)

It can be confirmed that financial and human resources are very important and strongly impact the successful adoption of any innovation in both large companies and SMEs. Specifically, in SMEs, it is necessary to have plentiful and long-term financial resource and the human resources with extensive knowledge in

> the field of application to ensure the successful application of the Balanced Scorecard. (CEO3)

Many companies in Vietnam made the mistake of assuming that having set up the indicator system, the goal is to complete the construction stage of the Balanced Scorecard and just wait for the evaluation. The goals will never be achieved if the business cannot identify the investment and action program and the plan for allocation of necessary resources.

Development stage of company

The effect of the development stage of a company on the adoption of the Balanced Scorecard in SMEs was explored in the Study 1. The developmental stage of a company influences the adoption of the Balanced Scorecard was once again confirmed in Study 2 by all interviewees.

> At the beginning of our business, we had no plan to apply the Balanced Scorecard or any other management models. We used all resources we must quickly find customers, dominate the market, and improve the turnover. Once achieving stability in business growth, we realized that the company needs to apply an effective performance management model such as the Balanced Scorecard to create the sustainability for long-term development. (CEO1)

Sharing the opinion of the director of a manufacturing SME, a Business Development Manager of the agribusiness SME asserted:

> The development stage of the business has a certain impact on the application of the Balanced Scorecard in the business. We have been developing our business for a while and realized that it was time to really start using the Balanced Scorecard to make good business strategies closely align the company's business objectives, and effectively manage the business operations. (BDM3)

It is very good to apply the Balanced Scorecard from the time of establishment of the company because this model can help the company to effectively promote their policies and strategies right from the start.

However, for start-up companies, especially SMEs, it is necessary to focus mainly on how the company can survive and thrive in new markets rather than to adopt a performance management tool when the company's operation is still unstable. From the discussions of the interviewees, the stable development stage of company was confirmed as the stage where SMEs think of the need to apply the Balanced Scorecard or any innovations for a better and sustainable development.

Organizational culture

The interviewees confirmed that organizational culture impacts the decision to adopt and the successful adoption of the Balanced Scorecard in companies, especially SMEs.

Initial template: Organizational culture	Final template: Organizational culture
Decentralization	Centralized commitment
Innovation	Innovation
Collaboration	Consensus and collaboration
Ready to take risks	Ready to take risks

Table 5.7 *Initial and final template of Organizational culture*

Decentralization

The results of Study 1 highlighted the impact of decentralization on the decision of to adopt the Balanced Scorecard in SMEs in Vietnam. The purpose of decentralization is to prevent the concentration of power in top managers and promote the role of all staff in the company in the adoption of the Balanced Scorecard. In contrast to the finding of Study 1, the interviewees of this study (Study 2) emphasized that a centralized commitment is the factor affecting the decision to adopt and the successful adoption of Balanced Scorecard in Vietnamese SMEs.

As mentioned in the top management factor, the CEO is the most important person in the decision to adopt the Balanced Scorecard in SMEs and leads the whole process of Balanced Scorecard adoption until its success. Ensuring the role of the CEO in the successful implementation of the Balanced Scorecard requires a centralized commitment. All members of the company need to comply with the requirements of the CEO to apply the Balanced Scorecard consistently and correctly.

> With seven years of Balanced Scorecard adoption, we can be sure that centralized commitment instead of decentralization will bring success to the application of Balanced Scorecard or any other modern management models in SMEs. On a small scale, implementing the Balanced Scorecard through intermediary management levels will increase the cost of time, finance and human resources, and sometimes the directions of the CEO will not be conveyed accurately. Instead, centralized commitment will direct the CEO's instructions to the staff and, in turn the employees' activities in the implementation of Balanced Scorecard will directly feedback to the CEO. From there, the CEO continues to make further decisions. (CEO1)

> It is necessary to have the help of all departments and staff in the company to successfully implement the Balanced Scorecard. For large companies, it requires decentralization to avoid being stuck at work. However, in SMEs, centralized commitment is a better option in that the CEO can directly manage each employee as well as monitors the process Balanced Scorecard implementation. Additionally, all staffs need to focus on executing the orders of the CEO so that the application of the Balanced Scorecard is uniform and not diverted. (CEO4)

> Decentralization helps to reduce the conceptualization of power on some individuals in the company. However, it sometimes also reduces the focus on prioritizing work. Functional departments can focus on solving their important tasks first instead of participating in the process of implementing the Balanced Scorecard. In contrast, the centralized commitment will require all members of the company to fully focus on the process of Balanced Scorecard application process until achieving its goals. (HRM2)

Most of the interviewees in Study 2 supported centralized commitment instead of decentralization as one of the organizational culture factors influencing the successful adoption of the Balanced Scorecard in Vietnamese SMEs.

> There will be many obstacles to fulfilling orders from the CEO and heads of departments at the same time. In order to achieve a unified process of adopting the Balanced Scorecard in SMEs, our company's experiences proved that it is advisable to unify the execution of the orders issued by the CEO. The CEO is the first person in SMEs to understand and decide to apply the Balanced Scorecard. They are also the main responsible person for the success or failure of the implementation. The implementation of the centralized commitment will create a unity in the application and operation of the Balanced Scorecard, ensuring the success of this process. (CEO2)

Innovation

The interviewees asserted that any business, large, medium, or small, with an innovation organizational culture, will be ready to apply innovation and achieve success from adopting the innovation.

> Positive thinking about innovation has created advantages for our company when adopting the Balanced Scorecard. We view the Balanced Scorecard as an essential innovation method that brings many benefits in our company's business development. While many companies consider the Balanced Scorecard to be a challenge because they do not have experience in the application of a modern management tool, our company with many experiences in innovation is ready to face the difficulties and challenges in applying the Balanced Scorecard by having a clear and detail adoption plan. (BDM3)

> We know it is not easy to apply the Balanced Scorecard successfully in a small-scale business like ours. However, with our creativity, and our interest in innovation, we have been actively learning about the Balanced Scorecard, adjusting the model to be

> able to fit the conditions of our company. It can be affirmed that if your business is an innovation-preferred enterprise, willing to apply innovation to achieve sustainable development, your business will successfully apply the Balanced Scorecard or any other performance management methods. (HRM1)

Consensus and collaboration

The findings of Study 1 showed that collaboration among company members is a favorable factor affecting the decision to adopt the Balanced Scorecard in SMEs. In this study (Study 2), the interviewees confirmed that the consensus and collaboration of all employees in the company will contribute to the success implementation of the Balanced Scorecard in Vietnamese SMEs.

> In order to have collaboration in an organization, it is necessary firstly to have a high level of consensus of its members. When deciding to apply the Balanced Scorecard to the company, we held many meetings to introduce the Balanced Scorecard, analyze the benefits that the company, and each member achieve when applying this model. We are willing to listen to and explain all the questions of members. Once there is a consensus among all members of the company, there will be a cooperation to implement the Balanced Scorecard. (CEO3)

> Consensus and collaboration are important factors impacting the success of Balanced Scorecard adoption or any other activities in a company. In SMEs, although the CEO is the most important person deciding all decisions in the company, it also requires the agreement and cooperation of all staff. The consensus and collaboration between top management and bottom-up can create all the success in a company. At the beginning of the Balanced Scorecard adoption in our company, we faced many difficulties because of disagreements among staff. Although they worked together to implement the Balanced Scorecard, it was an "unreal" collaboration. The staff worried

> that their benefit could be decreased, and their responsibility would be increased because of the new tasks and indicators of the Balanced Scorecard. We made clear explanations to our employees until we got the consensus. From that, a "real" collaboration has been built that made the process of the Balanced Scorecard adoption in our company runs smoothly. (CEO4)

Ready to take risks

From the interviewees' point of view, readiness to take risks is a key factor to the success of Balanced Scorecard adoption. Although this model has been proved an effective model for SMEs in theory and practice, inefficiencies can still occur when applied to specific SMEs. With this failure comes the loss of organizational resources. If SMEs are not ready to cope with expected risks, and are always afraid of failure, they will not be able to successfully adopt the Balanced Scorecard or any other innovations.

> We gave a lot of consideration on the decision to choose and apply the Balanced Scorecard because we worried about failure. However, with many experiences of facing the risks in previous projects, we decided to apply the Balanced Scorecard. After seven years of implementing this model, we realize that risks and failures always parallel successes. Being ready to take risks help us to prepare a plan to prevent risks in the process of applying this model. (CEO1)

> Preventing the expected risks that may occur when implementing a new project in the company, we proposed plans to minimize risks. We have learned carefully about the Balanced Scorecard from theory as well as practical experience from the Balanced Scorecard adopter SMEs. We have asked the support of a Balanced Scorecard consulting organization and of business networks. We hired experts to support the Balanced Scorecard application in the company at the beginning period. These activities cost us a big amount of money but in return, we were safe and convenient in the process of Balanced Scorecard adoption. (FM3)

Organizational strategy

Initial template: Organizational strategy	Final template: Organizational strategy
Continuous products/service improvement	Continuous products/service improvement
Innovation and development	Innovation and development

Table 5.8 *Initial and final template of Organizational strategy*

The Balanced Scorecard is a tool used in the strategic planning process to ensure the company's efforts are aligned with its overall strategy and vision. To apply the Balanced Scorecard requires enterprises to have an appropriate organizational strategy. In other words, organizational strategy has a great influence on the successful application of the Balanced Scorecard in enterprises. The findings of Study 2 have consistently confirmed an organizational strategy together with continuous product/service improvement, innovation, and development impact strongly on the process of Balanced Scorecard adoption in SMEs.

The Balanced Scorecard was designed to help enterprises assess their activities, not just with the financial perspective of using revenues, costs, and profits. It also presents a balanced view that considers other perspectives on success. The Balanced Scorecard effectively addresses the shortcomings of short-term financial measures and reflects past performance by adding measures that are the driving forces for future business development. Therefore, the successful adoption of the Balanced Scorecard in the company requires a long-term organizational strategy that focuses on quality of products and services improvement, and innovation for the sustainable development of the company.

> We desired to build a business strategy consistent with the policy of improving and developing products and services in the direction of innovation and sustainability. It is interesting that the Balanced Scorecard is a strategic management system to manage strategy in the long term. It helps us clarify and communicate our vision and strategy; communicate, link strategic goals and evaluation criteria; planning, setting goals,

linking strategic measures, and promoting strategic feedback and learning. (ITM2)

The Balanced Scorecard is a measurement system, information exchange tool, and strategic management system. Besides being a communication and measurement tool, the Balanced Scorecard is also considered a strategic management system because it is an important tool to adjust short-term and long-term activities by strategy. By using the Balanced Scorecard, organizations can restrict and eliminate barriers when implementing the strategy, including barriers to vision, barriers to people, barriers to resource allocation, and barriers to management. The Balanced Scorecard is very effective tool to help organizations build up business strategies. It is especially suitable for enterprises wishing to build business strategies towards long-term development, innovation, and sustainability. (CEO1)

Ownership

This study has consistently confirmed the findings of Study 1 on the role of ownership in the adoption of the Balanced Scorecard in SMEs. Privately-owned and other sectors of ownership (limited liability company, join stock company, etc.) were confirmed as the main sectors preferring to adopt the Balanced Scorecard to manage their performance. The interviewees thought that state-owned SMEs also needed to adopt the Balanced Scorecard for better development. However, the support of the government rendered state-owned SMEs unaware of the need to apply innovation to become stronger.

Initial template: Ownership	Final template: Ownership
Privately-owned	Privately-owned
Other sectors	Other sectors

Table 5.9 *Initial and final template of Ownership*

While state-owned companies receive a lot of Government's supports with policy, finance, law consulting, etc., we take

> responsibilities by ourselves. Once they encounter difficulties or a crisis, they receive the help in terms of capital and other resources from the State. Conversely, we solve all problems by our own. Therefore, we need to adopt a modern performance management system to help the company minimize the risks and get better development. The Balanced Scorecard could be a good consideration. The fact of several years of the Balanced Scorecard adoption at our company has proved it. (CEO1)

> Foreign-invested enterprises or subsidiaries of foreign enterprises have many advantages when applying the Balanced Scorecard because they have had many opportunities to access the Balanced Scorecard model in the other countries. In some cases, CEOs of these companies have been involved in the process of implementation of the Balanced Scorecard in previous enterprises. Their knowledge and experience would be of great help in applying the Balanced Scorecard at the current company. (BDM3)

5.3. Summary of results

Recently, the Balanced Scorecard has been considered a beneficial performance management model for both large companies and SMEs. However, most of the literature and empirical evidence has focused on the adoption and implementation of the Balanced Scorecard in large enterprises. There is a lack of research regarding the adoption of the Balanced Scorecard in SMEs, especially in the Vietnamese context. From the factors impacting the decision to adopt the Balanced Scorecard in SMEs derived from the literature review, the objective of Study 1 was to identify the factors affecting the decision to adopt the Balanced Scorecard in Vietnamese SMEs. The findings of Study 1 became the initial templates for the Study 2 case studies of four successful Balanced Scorecard adopter SMEs in different areas of Vietnam.

In comparison with the contingent factors derived from Contingency theory as the referent theoretical framework, the findings of Study 2 pointed out that although these contingent factors were considered as the main influences of the decision to adopt the Balanced Scorecard in other contexts, some of them were not seen to play an important role in the successful adoption of the Balanced Scorecard in Vietnamese SMEs. Due to the characteristics of Vietnamese SMEs, new impact factors appear to replace the role of some factors referred to in the literature. The new factors are (1) the focus on the CEO instead of the involvement of leadership that includes both top management and middle management, (2) the support from business networks instead of the support from local government, (3) the impact of regional differences between the north and the south of Vietnam, (4) organizational resources instead of firm size impact the successful adoption of the Balanced Scorecard, (5) an organizational culture focusing on innovation, centralized commitment, consensus and collaboration, and ready to take risks rather than focusing on the type of organizational culture, and (6) privately-owned or other types of ownership tend to adopt the Balanced Scorecard instead of all types of ownership. These findings support the idea of the contingency framework which offers reasonable explanations for different applications of performance measurement systems (Fakhri, 2012).

Study 2 showed that most of the factors impacting the decision to adopt the Balanced Scorecard in Vietnamese SMEs that were found in Study 1 also strongly influence the successful adoption of the Balanced Scorecard in Vietnamese SMEs. However, there were some differences in the results of Study 2 compared with the results of Study 1, which need to be highlighted. They are: (1) the focus on CEO instead of on top management in general, (2) differences between northern and southern regions instead of differences among all the regions, and (3) consensus and collaboration instead of collaboration only. The differences can be explained as the factors found in Study 1 may influence the decision to apply the Balanced Scorecard in Vietnamese SMEs but do not also impact the success of the adoption of this model in these enterprises. To be able to successfully adopt the Balanced Scorecard in the Vietnamese SMEs context, the findings of Study 2 require a detailed focus on top management, regional differences, and organizational culture.

Table 5.10 presents the final template developed from Study 2 in comparison with initial template formulated from the findings of Study 1 and contingency factors based on Contingency theory drawn from the literature review.

Contingency factors from literature review	Findings of Study 1	Findings of Study 2
Leadership (Braam & Nijssen, 2008; Hambrick & Mason, 1984; Hendricks et al., 2004; Murphy & Southey, 2003)	**Top management**	**CEO**
Top management involvement (Al-Omiri, 2003; Braam & Nijssen, 2008; Glaser et al., 2015; Volery et al., 2015) ***Top management support*** (Al-Omiri, 2003; Braam & Nijssen, 2008; Glaser et al., 2015; Volery et al., 2015) ***Senior management involvement*** (Bisbe & Barrubés, 2012; Chan, 2004; Inamdar et al., 2002)	Top management qualifications and awareness Top management commitment - Interdepartmental communication	Qualifications and awareness of CEO Commitment of CEO - Interdepartmental communication
External environment (Chenhall, 2003; Kaplan & Bruns, 1987)	**External environment**	**External environment**
The intensity of market competition (Abdel-Maksoud et al., 2005; Ahmad & Zabri, 2015; Chenhall & Morris, 1986; Luther & Longden, 2001; Mia & Clarke, 1999) ***The support of local government*** (Bertolini & Giovannetti, 2006; Meyer & Nguyen, 2005; Tran et al., 2009)	The intensity of market competition The support of business networks Differences among the regions	The intensity of market competition The support of business networks Differences between the northern and the southern regions

Contingency factors from literature review	Findings of Study 1	Findings of Study 2
Firm size (Ahmad & Zabri, 2015; Burns & Stalker, 1961; Chenhall, 2003; Fakhri, 2012; Hendricks et al., 2012; Hoque & James, 2000; Lawrence & Lorch, 1967; Liu et al., 2014; Oghuvwu & Omoye, 2016; Quesado et al., 2016; Speckbacher et al., 2003; Vo & Pham, 2018; Woodward, 1980)	**Organizational resources**	**Organizational resources**
Revenue (Hoque & James, 2000) ***Total assets*** (Hoque & James, 2000) ***Number of employees*** (Hoque & James, 2000)	Human and financial resources Development stages of company	Human and financial resources Development stages of company
Organizational Culture (Baird et al., 2004; Burns & Stalker, 1961; Chenhall, 2003; Chia & Koh, 2007; Henri, 2006; Kumar, 2001; Robbins, 2006)	**Organizational Culture**	**Organizational Culture**
Outcome orientation organizational culture (Kumar, 2001; Robbins, 2006) ***Innovation organizational culture*** (Kumar, 2001; Robbins, 2006) ***Team orientation organizational culture*** (Kumar, 2001; Robbins, 2006) ***Attention to details organizational culture*** (Kumar, 2001; Robbins, 2006)	Decentralization Innovation Collaboration Ready to take risks	Centralized commitment Innovation Consensus and Collaboration Ready to take risks

Contingency factors from literature review	Findings of Study 1	Findings of Study 2
Organizational Strategy (Bititci et al., 2012; Čater & Pučko, 2010; Chenhall, 2003; Dinh et al., 2018; Fakhri, 2012; Garengo & Biazzo, 2012; Garengo & Bititci, 2007; Hendricks et al., 2012; Liu et al., 2014; Vo & Pham, 2018)	**Organizational Strategy**	**Organizational Strategy**
Continuous product/services improvement (Braam & Nijssen, 2008; Danneels, 2002)	Continuous product/service improvement	Continuous product/service improvement
Innovation and development (Braam & Nijssen, 2008; Danneels, 2002)	Innovation and development	Innovation and development
Ownership (Darnall & Edwards Jr, 2006; Jensen & Meckling, 1976; Mascarenhas, 1989)	**Ownership**	**Ownership**
State-owned (Kaplan, 2001; Niven, 2008)	- Privately-owned	- Privately-owned
Privately-owned (Hoque, 2014)	Other sectors	Other sectors
Other sectors (Hoque, 2014)		

Table 5.10 *Study 2 Template*

Using template analysis, Study 2 answered the question of how the factors influence the successful adoption of the Balanced Scorecard by Vietnamese SMEs.

Firstly, top management was confirmed as the most important factor influencing the successful adoption of the Balanced Scorecard in Vietnamese SMEs. This study found that the CEO specifically plays a key role in the success of Balanced Scorecard adoption in Vietnamese SMEs. Unlike large companies with a big executive board, in SMEs, the CEOs take the main responsibility for all activities of the company, especially in the application of innovation, and throughout the entire management of the processes. This requires the appropriate qualifications and awareness of the CEOs as well as their commitment to innovation application. The successful adoption of the Balanced Scorecard in the four companies investigated in this study has demonstrated the significant influence of CEOs' qualifications, awareness, and commitment. Without these factors, the adoption may fail at the beginning. Interdepartmental communication in the enterprise also greatly affects the communication of the CEO's command to the staff and helps the CEO receive feedback from employees, contributing to the success in implementing the Balanced Scorecard in SMEs.

Secondly, this study has confirmed the considerable impact of external environmental factors on the adoption and application of Balanced Scorecard in Vietnamese SMEs. The intensity of market competition and the support of business networks control the Vietnamese SMEs' decision to adopt or not to adopt the Balanced Scorecard and the success or failure of the adoption process. The fiercer the competitive environment in which the SMEs operate, the keener they are to apply a modern management model to cope with difficulties, expand their market and develop businesses. Business networks, especially organizations and businesses that have experience in applying modern management tools, will greatly help SMEs to build and apply successful management models. This study showed that regional differences also have a significant impact on the successful adoption of the Balanced Scorecard of Vietnamese SMEs. However, while the differences were found between four regions in Study 1 (Southern, South-Central, Northern, and North-Central), Study 2 discovered differences only between the North and the South, while the Central regions exhibited similarities with their nearest neighboring region. While SMEs in the Southern areas adopt the Balanced Scorecard to achieve faster growth, SMEs in the Northern areas take safety as a top priority when deciding to apply Balanced Scorecard. Southern enterprises decide quickly to apply the Balanced Scorecard and promote its application in the SMEs sector while Northern enterprises are very cautious about applying it or any other innovation, which limits the number of SMEs applying the Balanced Scorecard in the Northern region.

Thirdly, the findings emphasized the importance of organizational resources in applying the Balanced Scorecard to SMEs. Thorough and long-term preparation of human and financial resources significantly contributes to the decision to adopt the Balanced Scorecard and its success in the business. This study confirmed that organizational resources, not firm size, affect the decision to adopt and the successful adoption of the Balanced Scorecard in SMEs, as long as the company has a team that is qualified and knowledgeable about the Balanced Scorecard, and well-prepared financial resources to meet all requirements of its application and long-term operation.

Finally, two new findings related to organizational culture emerged in this study. The literature review and Study 1 found that decentralization impacts the decision to adopt the Balanced Scorecard because it needs the help from top management, heads of departments and staff. Decentralization from top management to lower management levels is necessary so all staff in the company can contribute to the implementation process. Study 2 also confirmed the need for the contribution of all staff in the company for the successful adoption of the Balanced Scorecard. However, Study 2 focused mainly on the centralized commitment. In SMEs, the CEO is the most powerful person in all company decisions. Ensuring the success of the Balanced Scorecard adoption and implementation in SMEs requires centralized commitment. It is necessary for the CEO to fully use their powerful role, to focus on the ongoing management, monitoring and evaluation of the Balanced Scorecard application process. In addition, in order to implement the Balanced Scorecard successfully in Vietnamese SMEs, both consensus and collaboration are essential rather than merely cooperation, which, without consensus, is phony and does not achieve the expected results.

The results of Study 2 consistently confirmed that SMEs with the organizational strategy that focuses on the continued development and improvement of their products or services as well as on innovation will successfully apply the Balanced Scorecard. Additionally, the study also found that type of ownership influences the successful adoption of the Balanced Scorecard in SMEs. The findings showed that SMEs that are privately-owned or under other types of ownership tend to adopt the Balanced Scorecard more than state-owned SMEs. The ability to succeed in applying the Balanced Scorecard in these types of SMEs is much higher than in state-owned SMEs because autonomy in economic management requires non-state-owned SMEs to make efforts to preserve and develop their business on their own instead of waiting for the help from the State as state-owned SMEs do.

5.4. Conclusion

While Study 1 explored the factors impacting the decision of Vietnamese SMEs to adopt the Balanced Scorecard, Study 2 consisting of four successful Balanced Scorecard adopter case studies helped to answer the question of how the factors influence the successful adoption of the Balanced Scorecard in Vietnamese SMEs. The findings of this study contribute to a deeper understanding of the adoption/ non-adoption of the Balanced Scorecard by Vietnamese SMEs. These findings also contributed to the development of the instruments for the survey in the quantitative study (Study 3). The next chapter presents the details of the survey to test the hypotheses and confirm the factors affecting the level of adoption of the Balanced Scorecard in Vietnamese SMEs.

Chapter 6

What Are the Factors Affecting the Level of the Balanced Scorecard Adoption in Vietnamese Small and Medium Sized Enterprises?

6.1. Introduction

In Chapter 4 and Chapter 5, question 1 "Why have Vietnamese SMEs adopted or not adopted the Balanced Scorecard?" and question 2 "How do the factors influence the successful adoption of the Balanced Scorecard by Vietnamese SMEs?" were answered through the conduct of 32 individual interviews and four case studies. This chapter addresses question 3 "What are the factors affecting the level of the Balanced Scorecard adoption in Vietnamese SMEs?" From the results of the qualitative research (Studies 1 and 2), we identified a potential relationship between some external, internal and leadership factors and the level of the Balanced Scorecard adoption in Vietnamese SMEs. To investigate the relationship further, a conceptual framework with hypotheses was developed. A quantitative survey was undertaken with 1,500 SMEs that have adopted the Balanced Scorecard. 222 questionnaires were received from 1,500 respondents. Data were analyzed using SPSS statistical software. Test for normality was the first stage, followed by the Cronbach's Alpha method. Next, the Exploratory Factor Analysis (EFA) was applied and finally, the hypotheses were tested using the Regression Analysis model.

6.2. Conceptual Framework and Hypotheses

Taking the Contingency theory as the primary theory, Study 1 (in Chapter 3) and Study 2 (in Chapter 4) of this book discovered that top management, organizational strategy, organizational culture, organizational resources, the intensity of market competition, and the support from business networks are the main factors that impact the decision to adopt and the success of the adoption of the Balanced Scorecard in Vietnamese SMEs. Study 3, covered in this Chapter, through its use of the survey, took these factors as the main independent variables to examine their impact on the level of the Balanced Scorecard adoption in a sample of Balanced Scorecard-adopting SMEs in Vietnam. This section presents the hypotheses related to these variables.

Top management

Top management is considered one vital impact factor on the adoption of innovation and specifically on the adoption of management measures. Because of its dominant position in businesses, top management support and play a crucial role in an effective adoption (Kasperskaya, 2008; Kasurinen, 2002; Lueg & Vu, 2015; Phadtare, 2010). Kaplan and Norton (2008) mentioned top management as a main factor impacting the adoption of the Balanced Scorecard in any kinds of organization. Fernandes et al. (2006) highlighted the strong support from the top management in the successful implementation of the Balanced Scorecard in SMEs. The top management is the one who supplies the necessary resources, the professional project team, and participates in meetings related to the Balanced Scorecard implementation. The findings of Study 1 and Study 2 found a significant relationship between top management and the level of the Balanced Scorecard adoption in Vietnamese SMEs. Thus, the following hypothesis was developed:

H1: *Top management involvement has a positive impact on the level of the Balanced Scorecard adoption in Vietnamese SMEs.*

Organizational strategy

Kaplan and Norton (2008) emphasized strategy as the main element in the Balanced Scorecard adoption in an organization. When presenting the six steps of the Balanced Scorecard implementation, they focused on strategy as the first step that an organization needs to have in order to apply the Balanced Scorecard. Strategy has a vital impact on the design, adoption, and diffusion of innovation process (Chenhall, 2003; Fakhri, 2012; Hendricks et al., 2012). The findings of Study 1 and Study 2 confirmed that organizational strategy impacts the decision to adopt the Balanced Scorecard and its successful implementation in Vietnamese SMEs. It can be hypothesized that:

H2: *Organizational strategy has a positive impact on the level of the Balanced Scorecard adoption in Vietnamese SMEs.*

Organizational culture

The way an organization accepts innovation depends on their organizational culture (Oghuvwu & Omoye, 2016). Kaplan and Norton (2004) stressed the important role of organizational culture in the adoption of the Balanced Scorecard. Chenhall (2003) focused on organizational culture as a contingency factor impacting the adoption of management measurement system in an organization. Study 1 and Study 2 also suggested that an organizational culture featuring consensus and collaboration, readiness to take risks, and promoting innovation can affect the successful adoption of the Balanced Scorecard in Vietnamese SMEs. We aimed to confirm the relationship between organizational culture and the level of the Balanced Scorecard adoption in Vietnamese SMEs by proposing the following hypothesis:

H3: Organizational culture that supports collaboration has a positive impact on the level of the Balanced Scorecard adoption in Vietnamese SMEs.

Organizational resources

The findings of Study 1 discovered that organizational resources impact strongly on the Balanced Scorecard application in Vietnamese SMEs. This was also found in the related literature. Andon et al. (2007) found that Balanced Scorecard implementation in an organization requires well-prepared organizational resources because this process is long and complicate. Lueg and Vu (2015) confirmed the impact of organizational resources on the successful Balanced Scorecard application. Many Balanced Scorecard non-adopters indicated that organizational resources were the main reason for not adopting the Balanced Scorecard in their organizations (Perera et al., 2007). The relationship between organizational resources and adoption of the Balanced Scorecard leads to the following hypothesis:

H4: *Organizational resources have a positive impact on the level of the Balanced Scorecard adoption in Vietnamese SMEs.*

The intensity of market competition

The intensity of market competition has been revealed as an important factor that may affect the adoption of Balanced Scorecard in organizations (Dinh et al., 2018; Hoque & James, 2000; Malmi, 2001; Zuriekat, 2005). Hendricks et al. (2012) found that in Canada, Balanced Scorecard adopters were more impacted by market competition than non-adopters. Similarly, Ahmad and Zabri (2015), and Liu et al. (2014) discovered that the intensity of market competition has a significant correlation with the Balanced Scorecard adoption in organizations. Tran et al. (2007) confirmed that market competition is the main determinant of the adoption of new technology in Vietnamese SMEs. When the competition increases, businesses need to adopt a reliable performance measurement model to reinforce their operation. Additionally, the findings of Study 1 and Study 2 confirmed the influence of the intensity of market competition on the decision to adopt the Balanced Scorecard and the successful Balanced Scorecard adoption in Vietnamese SMEs. Thus, market competition as a relevant factor needs to be tested for its impact on the adoption of the Balanced Scorecard in Vietnamese SMEs. Therefore, the following hypothesis is derived:

H5: *The intensity of market competition has a positive impact on the level of the Balanced Scorecard adoption in Vietnamese SMEs.*

The support of business networks

Business networks are considered a good support for SMEs to achieve better development. Business networks can support SMEs to increase their capacity to access resources, technology, or information to approach the innovation (Evans et al., 2017; Premaratne, 2001). The support of business networks provides SMEs with new knowledge or access to the new knowledge creation process (Möller et al., 2005). Study 1 and Study 2 found a significant relationship between the support of business networks and the extent of the Balanced Scorecard adoption in Vietnamese SMEs. Thus, the following hypothesis was developed:

H6: *The support of business networks has a positive impact on the level of the Balanced Scorecard adoption in Vietnamese SMEs.*

Figure 6.1 illustrates the conceptual framework including the six variables that are hypothesized to influence the level of the Balanced Scorecard adoption in Vietnamese SMEs.

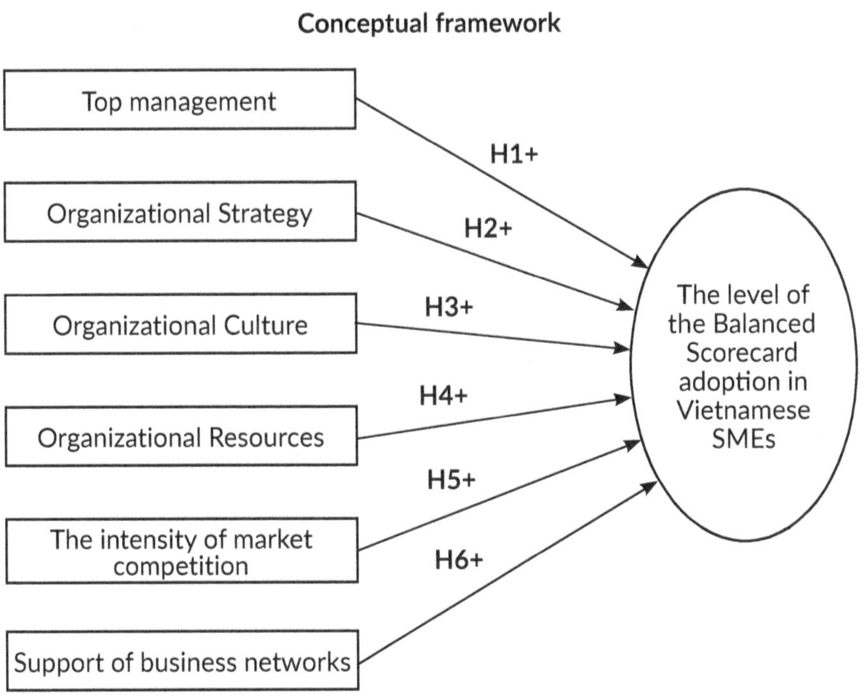

Source: Literature review and Researcher's compilation from the findings of Study 1 and Study 2

Figure 6.1: *Developed conceptual framework*

6.3. Description of the sample

Organization background

The participants for this quantitative study were the top managers of Vietnamese SMEs that have successfully adopted the Balanced Scorecard. These companies were identified from the list provided by the Vietnam Prosperity Joint Stock Commercial Bank. The Vietnam Prosperity Joint Stock Commercial Bank agreed to help with participant contacts and recruitment. 1,500 top managers of SMEs that had successfully adopted the Balanced Scorecard were contacted by emails to ask for their agreement to participate by completing a questionnaire. After obtaining the agreement of these top managers, the representative of Vietnam Prosperity Joint Stock Commercial Bank helped to complete the following steps: (1) distributing all questionnaires by email, (2) providing participants with clear explanations of information, (3) ensuring that while participation is encouraged, no-one is pressured to participate against their will, (4) collecting questionnaires in such a way that the individual's participation is anonymous and confidential, (5) transferring the questionnaire.

An email survey was used to collect the data because it can cover a large geographic area, has a large scale of distribution, and is time saving, and low cost (Zikmund, 2003). Moreover, an email survey is convenient for the respondents to complete from their place (Sekaran & Bougie, 1992; Sekaran & Bougie, 2003).

Participant demographics

222 questionnaires were received from 1,500 respondents, reaching a 14.8 percent response rate. All of the 222 questionnaires were usable. A summary of participant demographics is provided in Table 6.1.

Characteristics	Frequency	Percentage
Gender of business owner		
Male	145	64.3
Female	77	34.7
Age of business owner		
< 35	4	1.8
35 – 50	148	66.7
> 50	70	31.5
Qualifications of business owner		
≤ High School	1	0.5
Undergraduate	110	49.5
Postgraduate	111	50.0
Activity sector		
Agriculture, forestry, and fishery	77	34.7
Industry and construction	61	27.5
Trade and service	84	37.8
Type of ownership		
State-owned	32	14.4
Privately-owned	58	26.1
Joint stock company	67	30.2
Limited liability	65	29.3
Year of operation		
Less than 1 year	0	0
1 – 5 years	59	26.6
More than 5 years	163	73.4
Company location		
In the Southern area	76	34.2
In the Central area	64	28.8
In the Northern area	82	36.9
Time to adopt the Balanced Scorecard		
Less than 1 year	33	14.9
1 – 5 years	126	56.8
More than 5 years	63	28.4

Table 6.1: *Characteristics of the participants (N = 222)*

The survey reported that 64.3 percent of respondents were male, and 34.7 percent were female. These figures showed that approximately one-third of respondents are women-owned SMEs. This ratio is reasonable because the "Women in Business 2019" report of Thornton (2019) discovered that 36 percent of management positions in Vietnamese businesses are women.

Age of business owner was included in the sample. 1.8 percent of respondents were under 35 years old, 66.7 percent were from 35 to 50 years old, and 31.5 percent were over 50 years old.

Qualifications of business owner were also considered as a criterion in the sample structure. The survey reported that 50 percent of participants had postgraduate qualifications, 49.5 percent were at the undergraduate level, and only 0.5 percent was at the high school level.

34.7 percent of respondents were in agriculture, forestry, and fishery SMEs, 27.5 percent in industry and construction SMEs, and 37.8 in trade and service SMEs.

The sample structure by type of ownership was presented by 14.4 percent of respondents from state-owned SMEs, 26.1 percent were privately-owned SMEs, 30.2 percent were Joint stock companies, and 29.3 percent were limited liability companies.

Age of company was included in the sample. There was no respondent in a company that was less than one year in operation. 26.6 percent of companies were from 1 to 5 years of operation and 73.4 percent were more than five years of operation.

The location of the company was also considered in the sample. There was a balance among the respondents from three regions of Vietnam. 34.2 percent of the respondents were in Southern provinces, 28.8 percent were in Central provinces, and 36.9 percent were in Northern provinces.

All the respondents came from the Balanced Scorecard adopted SMEs; therefore, time having adopted the Balanced Scorecard was included in the sample. 14.9 percent of the respondents were less in than 1 year of the Balanced Scorecard adoption, 56.8 percent were from 1 to 5 years of the Balanced Scorecard adoption, and 28.4 percent were over 5 years.

6.4. Data analysis

The data were analysed using SPSS statistical software. Testing for normality was conducted in the first stage, followed by determination of Cronbach's Alpha. After that, Exploratory Factor Analysis (EFA) was applied before the hypotheses were tested using the Regression Analysis model.

Test for Normality

Results indicate that scale values, ranging from 1 to 5, fluctuate around the centre value of 3 and have the standard deviation value of around 0.7. In addition, the values for Skewness between -0.8 to 0.8 and Kurtosis between -2 to 2 are acceptable (George and Mallery, 2010). These results imply that the scales have a normal distribution, and, hence, are suitable for subsequent tests.

Reliability Analysis

The six variables of level of the Balanced Scorecard adoption, top management, organizational strategy, organizational resources, the intensity of market competition and the support of business networks provide high reliability with Cronbach's alpha above 0.7 and their items achieve the corrected item-total correction above 0.4 (Field, 2013). Meanwhile, organizational culture was tested twice resulting in the rejection of two items (believes in the importance of innovation and encourages risk taking), as their corrected item-total correlations were below 0.4.

Exploratory Factor Analysis

EFA was applied to evaluate the convergent value and discriminant value of the scale (Osborne et al., 2008). The results show that the factor analysis model is suitable (0.5 < KMO = 0.711 < 1); there are no relationships among variables (Sig. = 0.000 < 0.05); 22 variables are extracted into seven factors with total variance explaining 72.409% (eigenvalues of all factors> 1); the observed variables have factor loading greater than 0.5. That is, the requirements for factor analysis are met.

Correlation Analysis

After conducting an EFA analysis, the next step is to create a representative variable for each group of factors and conduct correlation analysis, regression analysis. Before performing the regression test, it is necessary to conduct the correlation analysis between the independent and dependent factors. The purpose of correlation analysis is to examine the close linear correlation between the dependent variable and the independent variables and early to identify the multicollinearity problem when the independent variables are strongly correlated with each other.

Hypothesis testing - Regression Analysis

The aforementioned analysis results confirm that there are six factors affecting the level of the Balanced Scorecard adoption in SMEs in Vietnam. These factors, in the next step, will be used as explanatory variables for the regression analysis model. This is the key step taken to test the hypotheses in the research model as well as answer the research question of *"What are the factors affecting the level of the Balanced Scorecard adoption in Vietnamese SMEs?"*

Proposed model:

$$Y = f(x) = \beta_0 + \beta_1 X_1 + \beta_2 X_2 + \beta_3 X_3 + \beta_4 X_4 + \beta_5 X_5 + \beta_6 X_6 + \varepsilon$$

in which:

Y: Level of the Balanced Scorecard adoption

X_1: Top management

X_2: Organizational strategy

X_3: Organizational culture

X_4: Organizational resources

X_5: The intensity of market competition

X_6: The support from business networks

β_0: constant

$\beta_1, \beta_2, \beta_3, \beta_4, \beta_5, \beta_6$: regression coefficient

ε: random error

In this research, Adjusted R-squared is 0.526. This result means that six independent variables explain about 52.6% of the change of the dependent variable. Durbin – Watson is used to check the correlation of adjacent errors. In this case, the Durbin – Watson of 1.777 means that there is no superlative sequence correlation in the model.

Model	R	R-squared	Adjusted R-squared	Std. Error of the Estimate	Durbin-Watson
1	.746a	.556	.526	.667	1.777
a. Predictors: (Constant), Company location, RES, CUL, STRA, SUPPORT, LEADER, COMPETTITION, gender, Type of ownership, Activity Sector, Characteristic - Qualifications, Year of operation, Characteristic - Age, Company location					
b. Dependent Variable: Level of the Balanced Scorecard adoption					

Table 6.2 *Model summary*

In addition, Table 6.3 also shows that five control variables of company location, gender of business owner, qualifications of business owner, age of business owner, and activity sector have a statistical significance to control the explanation of the variation of the dependent variable. Their statistical significance Sig. are under 0.05 (respectively: 0.01, 0.044, 0.00, 0.00, 0.017).

Model		Unstandardized Coefficients		Standardized Coefficients	t	Sig.	Collinearity Statistics	
		B	Std. Error	Beta			Tolerance	VIF
1	(Constant)	3.044	.452		6.740	.000		
	Activity Sector	.132	.055	.116	2.403	.017	.916	1.092
	Type of ownership	.038	.045	.041	.852	.395	.923	1.084
	Year of operation	.112	.109	.054	1.031	.304	.788	1.270
	Characteristic - Age	.389	.098	.204	3.977	.000	.814	1.228
	Characteristic - Qualification	-.379	.094	-.200	-4.031	.000	.874	1.144
	TOP MANAGEMENT	.117	.046	.120	2.508	.013	.932	1.074
	COMPETTITION	-.090	.048	-.093	-1.864	.064	.869	1.150
	SUPPORT	.163	.047	.168	3.459	.001	.911	1.098
	STRATEGY	.041	.047	.043	.887	.376	.922	1.084
	CULTURE	.215	.049	.222	4.422	.000	.849	1.178
	RESOURCES	.487	.048	.503	10.170	.000	.877	1.140
	gender	.205	.101	.101	2.023	.044	.866	1.155
	Company location	-.426	.124	-.213	-3.451	.001	.563	1.775
	Company location	-.403	.121	-.198	-3.326	.001	.606	1.652

a. Dependent Variable: Level of the Balanced Scorecard adoption

Table 6.3: Coefficients

6.5. Finding and Discussion

The results of data analysis are presented in Table 6.4. The results confirm that hypotheses H1, H3, H4, and H6 are not rejected. However, H2 and H5 are rejected by the data analysis.

Hypothesis	Relationship	Finding
Hypothesis 1	Top management → the level of the Balanced Scorecard adoption	Supported
Hypothesis 2	Organizational strategy → the level of the Balanced Scorecard adoption	Non-supported
Hypothesis 3	Organizational culture → the level of the Balanced Scorecard adoption	Supported
Hypothesis 4	Organizational resources → the level of the Balanced Scorecard adoption	Supported
Hypothesis 5	The intensity of market competition → the level of the Balanced Scorecard adoption	Non-supported
Hypothesis 6	The support from business networks → the level of the Balanced Scorecard adoption	Supported

Table 6.4: *Results of hypothesis testing*

Hypothesis H1 stated that *Top management has a positive impact on the level of the Balanced Scorecard adoption in Vietnamese SMEs.* The results show the relationship between top management and the level of the Balanced Scorecard adoption in Vietnamese SMEs has the value of Beta of 0.120 and statistical significance Sig. of 0.013 < 0.05 (Table 6.3). This confirms that the involvement and commitment of top management have a significant impact on the level of the Balanced Scorecard adoption in Vietnamese SMEs. With top management support and commitment to participate, the process of adoption and implementation of the Balanced Scorecard is easier and more advantaged.

Hypothesis H3 stated that *Organizational culture has a positive impact on the level of the Balanced Scorecard adoption in Vietnamese SMEs.* The value of Beta is 0.222 and statistical significance Sig. is 0.000 < 0.05 (Table 6.3). These figures show that the level of the Balanced Scorecard adoption in Vietnamese SMEs is influenced by organizational culture. An SME with a rich culture of innovation, collaboration, and exchange of ideas promotes the extent of the Balanced Scorecard use in their organizations.

Hypothesis H4 stated that *Organizational resources have a positive impact on the level of the Balanced Scorecard adoption in Vietnamese SMEs.* The results show that the relationship between organizational resources and the level of the Balanced Scorecard adoption in Vietnamese SMEs has the value of Beta of 0.503 and statistical significance Sig. of 0.000 < 0.05 (Table 6.3). With this result, the hypothesis is supported. This is a significant relationship because it has the highest value of Beta in comparison with the Beta of the other factors. This result confirms that the level of the Balanced Scorecard adoption in Vietnamese SMEs depends on the level of resources they prepare for the adoption. A thorough preparation of human resources, finance, and experts in the field of the Balanced Scorecard can help SMEs apply the Balanced Scorecard better and more effectively.

Hypothesis H6 stated that *The support of business networks has a positive impact on the level of the Balanced Scorecard adoption in Vietnamese SMEs.* The results of data analysis show that the relationship between the support of business networks and the level of the Balanced Scorecard adoption in Vietnamese SMEs has the value of Beta of 0.168 and statistical significance Sig. of 0.000 < 0.05 (Table 6.3). This result supports hypothesis H6. The more technical support and experiential advice support that SMEs receive from business networks, Balanced Scorecard adopters, and external consultants, the higher Balanced Scorecard adoption level in SMEs.

From the literature and previous studies, organizational strategy and the intensity of market competition have been considered as impact factors for SMEs to adoption the innovation. However, the results of this study do not confirm there is an impact on the level of the Balanced Scorecard adoption in Vietnamese SMEs because their Sig. are 0.376 and 0.064 respectively (Table 6.3).

From the results, the regression model in this study is drawn as follow:

$$Y = f(x) = 0.120X_1 + 0.222X_3 + 0.503X_4 + 0.168X_6$$

in which:

Y: Level of the Balanced Scorecard adoption

X_1: Top management

X_3: Organizational culture

X_4: Organizational resources

X_6: The support from business networks

Furthermore, the results of data analysis show that the level of the Balanced Scorecard adoption in Vietnamese SMEs has been impacted by company location, gender of business owner, qualifications of business owner, age of business owner, and activity sector.

Firstly, the results of Study 1 and Study 2 investigated whether regional differences impact the Balanced Scorecard adoption in Vietnamese SMEs. The Study 3 found that the relationship between company location and the level of the Balanced Scorecard adoption in Vietnamese SMEs has the statistical significance Sig. of 0.01 < 0.05 (Table 6.3). This result consistently confirms the influence of regional differences on the adoption of the Balanced Scorecard in SME in Vietnam.

Secondly, the results of data analysis reveal that the statistical significance of gender, qualifications, and age of business owner explain the variation of the level of the Balanced Scorecard adoption in Vietnamese SMEs. Business owners of different genders, ages, and qualifications make different decisions about adopting the Balanced Scorecard in their companies.

Finally, with the statistical significance Sig. of 0.017 < 0.05 (Table 6.3), activity sector is also proved to impact the level of the Balanced Scorecard adoption in Vietnamese SMEs.

These findings show that further research is required to examine more deeply the relationship between the level of the Balanced Scorecard adoption in Vietnamese SMEs and company location, gender of business owner, qualifications of business owner, age of business owner, and activity sector.

6.6. Summary of results

Vietnamese SMEs are unique and little research has been undertaken on the Balanced Scorecard adoption. This present research used a sequential mixed method design to explore the determinants of the Balanced Scorecard adoption in Vietnamese SMEs. The semi-structured interviews and case studies were conducted firstly as the exploratory studies to discover the factors that impact the decision of Vietnamese SMEs to adopt the Balanced Scorecard and how these factors impact their successful adoption. Finally, the results of this quantitative study (Study 3) identified the factors affecting the level of the Balanced Scorecard adoption in Vietnamese SMEs.

The statistical description presented participant demographics: gender, age, and qualifications of business owner, field of activity, type of ownership, years of operation, company location, and time to adopt the Balanced Scorecard. The results of scale tests were satisfactory. The results of the Cronbach's Alpha test met the requirements after removing two items from the organizational culture variable. The results of EFA were reasonable. The results of hypothetical testing accepted four of the six hypotheses that were initially proposed. These lead to the conclusion that four factors affected the level of the Balanced Scorecard adoption in Vietnamese SMEs.

This study (Study 3) found that the level of resources a Vietnamese SME has available in preparation impacts significantly on the level of the Balanced Scorecard adoption. Organizational resources are the most influential factor of the four factors. The process of Balanced Scorecard adoption involves much financial and non-financial input. This is different from the contingency variable of firm size that was considered a main factor to decide to adopt and successfully adopt the Balanced Scorecard in organizations.

The second most influential factor on the level of the Balanced Scorecard adoption in Vietnamese SMEs found in this study is organizational culture. The more an SME has the characteristics of promoting innovation and collaboration and exchange of ideas, the greater the extent of the Balanced Scorecard they adopt. This finding supports an innovate and collaborate organizational culture that were found in Study 1 and Study 2 for a successful adoption of the Balanced Scorecard in Vietnamese SMEs.

The next finding of this study confirmed the impact of the support of business networks on the level of the Balanced Scorecard adoption in Vietnamese SMEs. Besides the efforts of enterprises, the support from business networks has a great impact on the Balanced Scorecard adoption in SMEs. Business networks can support SMEs to increase their capacity to access resources, technology, or information to undertake innovation (Evans et al., 2017; Premaratne, 2001). This finding is intriguing and requires further research for a better understanding of the relationship between the support of business networks and the Balanced Scorecard in the SMEs context.

Finally, the finding of this study was consistent with the findings of Study 1 and Study 2 that top management makes the most important contribution to the decision, success, and the extent of the Balanced Scorecard adoption in Vietnamese SMEs. The kind of top management that can impact strongly on the level of the Balanced Scorecard adoption in Vietnamese SMEs is (1) very involved in introducing performance monitoring throughout the company, (2) understands that the company's key processes using indicators and criteria are essential to the company's success, and (3) well informed and supports every attempt to improve the company's performance.

6.7. Conclusion

Chapter 6 presents the research hypotheses developed from Study 1 and Study 2, the sample description, data analysis and results of the quantitative study to identify the factors affecting the level of the Balanced Scorecard adoption in Vietnamese SMEs. Chapter 7 presents the main inferences connecting the qualitative and quantitative studies, the contributions, the limitations of the research and the suggestions for further research.

Chapter 7

Discussion and Conclusion

7.1. Introduction

Using a sequential mixed method design, this research examined the factors that influenced the adoption of the Balanced Scorecard in Vietnamese SMEs. Vietnamese SMEs are unique, and there is little research on their adoption of the Balanced Scorecard. Mixed methods research designs have been considered good practice because the phenomena can be examined from multiple viewpoints, perspectives, positions and standpoints (Creswell & Plano Clark, 2011a; Johnson et al., 2007; Mathison, 1988). This research was conducted in the form of three studies comprising semi-structure interviews, four case studies, and a survey to address the three research questions. Study 1 found the reasons why Vietnamese SMEs have adopted or not adopted the Balanced Scorecard. Study 2 addressed the impact factors and the way these factors affect the successful adoption of the Balanced Scorecard in Vietnamese SMEs. Study 3 explored the factors that impact the level of the Balanced Scorecard adoption in Vietnamese SMEs. Contingency theory was used to underpin the research.

This chapter discusses the key findings and presents the resulting conclusions in response to the overall research problem of what the factors are influencing the successful adoption of the Balanced Scorecard in Vietnamese SMEs. This chapter also outlines the contributions of the research, its limitations, and the suggestions for further research.

7.2. Discussion of Main Findings

Question 1: ***Why have SMEs in developing countries adopted or not adopted the Balanced Scorecard?***

The Balanced Scorecard was first designed for use in large companies and has matured in developed countries (Oghuvwu & Omoye, 2016).

However, many researchers have confirmed that the Balanced Scorecard could be applied successfully in SMEs (Kaplan & Norton, 1996; Mahshid Lonbani et al., 2014). Recently, use of the Balanced Scorecard in SMEs has spread to Asian countries (Hussin & Yusoff, 2013; Sorooshian et al., 2016). In Vietnam, the Balanced Scorecard has been proposed as a crucial choice of performance measurement tool for Vietnamese SMEs to guarantee stable growth and a successful future (Tran, 2013). It is necessary to discover the factors that impact on the Balanced Scorecard adoption to promote widespread use of the Balanced Scorecard in Vietnamese SMEs. However, there is little research in this area.

In addressing Question 1, we discovered three groups of factors that affect the decision to adopt or not adopt the Balanced Scorecard in Vietnamese SMEs. These are external environmental factors, organizational factors, and leadership factors. The findings of this research confirmed the impact of market competition, organizational culture, organizational strategy, and type of ownership as found in previous research on the decision to adopt the Balanced Scorecard. Some important additional factors were considered.

Firstly, the literature review on the Balanced Scorecard research revealed that the level of market competition is an important factor that may affect the usage of the Balanced Scorecard (Hoque & James, 2000; Malmi, 2001). Businesses need to act to the best of their abilities in dealing with market competition (Ashurst & Doherty, 2003). Maiga and Jacobs (2003) supported the implementation of the Balanced Scorecard in business to respond to the competitive environment. This present research found that Vietnamese SMEs facing greater competitive pressure are more likely to adopt the Balanced Scorecard to provide them with a suitable strategic plan to deal with market fluctuations. These companies "take" intensity of market competition as an opportunity to look for best performance management practices and enhance their capabilities.

Secondly, the research found that the differences among the regions in Vietnam was an external environmental factor that impacts the decision of the Balanced Scorecard adoption in Vietnamese SMEs. This is a noteworthy finding, requiring further research on the use of the Balanced Scorecard and on the adoption of other innovations in Vietnamese SMEs. Historically, during the time that Southern Vietnam was occupied by the United State of America, it followed capitalism, while Northern Vietnam belonged to the Democratic Republic of Vietnam and followed a centralized economic model. The finding shows that SMEs in the Southern and South-Central provinces are willing to adopt and implement the Balanced Scorecard quickly while SMEs in the Northern and North-Central provinces are more conservative in making decisions, especially in adopting innovative applications. Much of the research on the Balanced Scorecard in South East Asia assumes in-country consistency of the culture and business contexts. The result of this current study highlights the importance of intracultural differences when examining business processes (Fisher & Härtel, 2004).

Thirdly, according to the literature, the support of local government is an important factor for SMEs in adopting the new technologies to improve their businesses (Nguyen et al., 2017; Vo, 2015). However, this present research found that the support of local government does not affect Vietnamese SMEs' decision to apply the Balanced Scorecard. Rather, their decision is influenced by the support of the business networks. To adopt the Balanced Scorecard, Vietnamese SMEs receive great support from the SMEs Associations which organize seminars and workshops to present and exchange both theoretical and practical information about of the Balanced Scorecard. They also get the technical support and experiential advice from successful Balanced Scorecard adopters and external consultants. Colclough et al. (2019) indicated that having the support of a business network is important in the implementation of innovation strategies of SMEs.

Another new finding of this present research is that firm size has no influence on the decision to adopt the Balanced Scorecard in Vietnamese SMEs whereas previous research indicated that firm size was a factor (Ahmad & Zabri, 2015; Chenhall, 2003; Oghuvwu & Omoye, 2016; Quesado et al., 2016; Speckbacher et al., 2003). The findings of Study 1 show that in Vietnam, enterprises of any scale can adopt the Balanced Scorecard depending on the development stage of the enterprise and the level of organizational resources they have available to prepare for the adoption. This finding provides the opportunity for further research on the adoption of the Balanced Scorecard in SMEs with the limitation of firm size.

Another significant factor influencing the decision to adopt or reject a performance measurement system is type of ownership (Doan et al., 2011; Le & Harvie, 2010; Smith, 2010). At the beginning of this present research, Study 1 proposed that all types of ownership have an impact on the Balanced Scorecard adoption in Vietnamese SMEs. However, the findings of the study showed that while privately-owned and other types of ownership (joint stock companies, limited liability companies, foreigner companies, etc.) are willing to adopt the Balanced Scorecard, state-owned companies are not. Unlike the state-owned companies, the other types of ownership-based companies do not receive many incentives from the State and need to innovate to survive in the fierce competitive environment. State-owned is not the type of ownership that encourages the adoption of the Balanced Scorecard in Vietnamese SMEs. Their capital has been allocated annually by the State; their activities need to approval from the State; they follow the action plan directed by the State. The interviewees do not think the Balanced Scorecard is necessary in their companies.

Organizational culture was considered an important contingent factor impacting the adoption of the Balanced Scorecard and other performance measurement systems in previous research (Asiaei & Jusoh, 2014; Chenhall, 2003; Kaplan & Norton, 2004; Oghuvwu & Omoye, 2016). At the beginning of this present research, Study 1 proposed that types of organizational culture, including (1) outcome orientation, (2) innovation, (3) team orientation, (4) detail orientation, impact the decision to adopt or not adopt the Balanced Scorecard in Vietnamese SMEs. The findings of Study 1 found that an organizational culture with decentralization, innovation, collaboration, and readiness to take risks that embraces the characteristics of the above types of impact significantly the decision to adopt the Balanced Scorecard in Vietnamese SMEs.

The last finding of this research is related to leadership. The literature suggests that top and senior management involvement provides the leadership that impacts the adoption of the Balanced Scorecard of SMEs (Baird et al., 2007; Braam & Nijssen, 2008). However, in the Vietnamese context, the qualifications and commitment of top management are the most important factors in the direction of the enterprise to adopt or not to adopt the Balanced Scorecard. The director of a Vietnamese SME is the only person who understands and decides to implement new technologies in the company. It is necessary to have the intense involvement of top management in determining and monitoring key indicators. Day-to-day supervision of top management keeps the adoption of the Balanced Scorecard on track (Phadtare, 2010). Senior management assists the director and tends to be involved in the management and implementation of the Balanced Scorecard.

Question 2: ***How do the factors influence the successful adoption of the Balanced Scorecard by SMEs in developing countries?***

The findings of Study 1 provided the initial themes for Study 2 which addressed question 2. Study 2 offered several findings in response to question 2.

Firstly, regional differences have been consistently found to impact the adoption of Balanced Scorecard in Vietnamese SMEs. The findings of Study 2 confirmed that the successful adoption of Balanced Scorecard in Vietnamese SMEs is affected by the differences between the Northern regions and Southern regions of Vietnam but not by differences between the Central provinces and the Northern and Southern provinces. While Southern and South-Central SMEs tend to be open to innovation for the purpose of increasing their profit, Northern and North-Central SMEs take safety as the top priority in all their decisions. These different priorities shape the process and success of Balanced Scorecard implementation in SMEs in Vietnam, their focus being the values that the Balanced Scorecard offers. The Southern SMEs with their main rapid growth-oriented focus will be interested in successful adoption of the Balanced Scorecard in order to achieve better development. The Northern SMEs emphasize security much more than challenges. They will try to successfully apply the Balanced Scorecard to achieve a sustainable growth and ensure safety in business development.

Secondly, the findings of this study have consistently affirmed the strong influences of the intensity of market competition and the support of business networks as the external environmental factor on the successful adoption of the Balanced Scorecard in Vietnamese SMEs. To respond to the restrictions of the competitive business environment, successful businesses need to adopt the Balanced Scorecard to assist in their management processes by coordinating the involvement of suppliers, customers, and employees. The support of business networks also provides knowledge of how to respond to the pressures of competition. This support can help Vietnamese SMEs save resources and shorten the time to achieve success in business management. Vietnamese SMEs can avoid the failures and design a reasonable plan for the adoption of the Balanced Scorecard by learning from the experiences of the network of business that have already adopted the Balanced Scorecard.

Thirdly, the role of top management in the adoption and implementation of the Balanced Scorecard has been mentioned and confirmed by many previous studies. The findings of this present research confirmed this phenomenon in the Vietnamese SME context. Regardless of the environment, the innovation process is initiated and led by the top management. They are the persons who create the motivation and have the determination to lead the innovation to success. In the SME context, the CEO, not the executive board, is the most powerful person and decides all activities of the enterprise. The findings of this research focus on the qualifications and awareness of the CEO as well as their commitment as key to the success of the adoption of the Balanced Scorecard in Vietnamese SMEs. In addition, the findings of Study 1 and Study 2 also accept that a good interdepartmental communication in a SME supports the Balanced Scorecard adoption by supporting the top manager in his/her role in directing, monitoring, and supervising the process of the adoption. A close association among the members of the company ensures the information system is transferred transparently and in a timely way.

Next, organizational culture also contributes significantly to the successful adoption of the Balanced Scorecard in Vietnamese SMEs. The finding of the CEO as the decision maker in the successful adoption of the Balanced Scorecard in Vietnamese SMEs led to the further finding regarding commitment to centralization. To ensure the CEO's power is focused, a commitment to centralization is essential. Previous research shows that centralized commitment with its rigid and authoritarian principles could prevent the innovation process. Top managers should give decision making authority to lower level employees to get quick action and flexibility. However, to maximize the CEO's power in making decisions and directing the implementation process to achieve the success of Balanced Scorecard in Vietnamese SMEs, centralized commitment is a requirement. On the other hand, for successful implementation, it is also necessary to have consensus and collaboration, rather than just the total cooperation of the members of the business. Cooperation without consensus is mere semblance and does not achieve the expected results.

The findings of Study 2 indicated that state-owned companies do not adopt the Balanced Scorecard, while privately-owned and other types of ownership SMEs have the Balanced Scorecard as their preference form of performance management. The participants of Study 2 agreed with the idea that all types of ownership need to adopt the Balanced Scorecard. However, they showed that the support of government leads state-owned SMEs miss the chance to adopt the Balanced Scorecard for better development.

Finally, this research consistently confirmed that organizational resources, and organizational strategy are keys to the decision to adopt the Balanced Scorecard. Regardless of the firm size, a SME with well-prepared resources can successfully adopt and implement the Balanced Scorecard approach. Additionally, the development stage of a SME also contributes to the potentiality of the success or failure of the adoption of the Balanced Scorecard in its company: a SME in the stable development stage rather than a start-up company needs to apply the Balanced Scorecard for a sustainable growth. The percentage of success in these companies is higher than in start-up companies. Organizational strategy also contributes significantly to the success of Balanced Scorecard adoption in Vietnamese SMEs. Such strategies involve continuous product/service improvement, innovation, and development, ensuring a SME's efforts are aligned with its overall strategy and vision.

Question 3: ***What are important factors affecting the level of the Balanced Scorecard adoption in SMEs in developing countries?***

Based on the findings of Study 1 and Study 2, Study 3 addressed question 3 with hypotheses for the six factors of *top management, organizational strategy, organizational culture, organizational resources, the intensity of market competition,* and *the support of business networks*. In addition, the seven control variables of company location, years of operation, activity sector, type of ownership, gender, age, and qualifications of business owner were added in the regression analysis. The results of data analysis confirmed four of the six factors impact positively the level of the Balanced Scorecard adoption in SMEs in Vietnam. They are (1) *top management,* (2) *organizational culture,* (3) *organizational resources,* and (4) *the support of business networks*. Three factors of top management, organizational culture, and organizational resources were mentioned in literature and previous research as impacting the adoption and implementation of the Balanced Scorecard by different type of organizations in different national and cultural contexts. The findings of this present research consistently support the key role of these factors on the Balanced Scorecard adoption in Vietnam. However, this present research found the support of business networks as the new factor that impacts the Balanced Scorecard adoption. Although previous research supported the impact of business networks on SMEs' development (Berry et al., 2006; Clifton et al., 2010; Major & Cordey-Hayes, 2000; Zain & Ng, 2006), the relationship between this factor and the Balanced Scorecard adoption in SMEs is largely under-researched. This research, therefore, makes a novel contribution to the relevant literature by adding this new factor to the list of determinants of the Balanced

Scorecard adoption among SMEs.

Regarding other factors that may affect the level of the Balanced Scorecard adoption in Vietnamese SMEs, seven control variables of company location, years of operation, activity sector, type of ownership, gender, age, and qualifications of business owner were added in the regression analysis. The results indicated that company location, gender of business owner, qualifications of business owner, age of business owner, and activity sector provided statistically significant explanations to the variation of the level of the Balanced Scorecard adoption.

Of the four factors impacting on the level of the Balanced Scorecard adoption found in this research, organizational resources are the most influential one with the value of Beta at 0.503. The second most influential factor is organizational culture with Beta at 0.222. This means that resources and culture play very important roles in SME operation, especially in innovation and the Balanced Scorecard adoption. It was argued in the literature that organizational resources are the main reason for adopting or not adopting the Balanced Scorecard in an organization (Perera et al., 2007). The adoption of the Balanced Scorecard is a long-term and multi-steps process that need to have very well prepared financial and human resources as well as the advice of Balanced Scorecard experts. In addition, the more the SMEs are interested in innovation, are willing to take risks and exchange ideas, and feature a collaboration culture, the greater the extent of adoption of the Balanced Scorecard in their business.

Top management and the support of business networks also impact significantly on the level of the Balanced Scorecard adoption in Vietnamese SMEs. Top management and the support of the business networks are always designated as the important factors in the decision to adopt, the success, and the extent of the Balanced Scorecard adoption in Vietnamese SMEs. The kind of top management that (1) is very much involved in introducing performance monitoring throughout the company, (2) understands that a company's key processes using indicators and criteria are essential to the company's success, and (3) is well informed and supports every attempt to improve the company's performance, can impact strongly on the successful adoption of the Balanced Scorecard in Vietnamese SMEs. In addition, receiving technical support and the experiential advice from Balanced Scorecard adopters, from networks and from consultants encourages SMEs to feel more confident to adopt the Balanced Scorecard.

The overarching problem: ***What are the factors influencing successful adoption of the Balanced Scorecard in SMEs in developing countries?***

The key purpose of the research was to explore the determinants of successful Balanced Scorecard adoption by SMEs in developing countries, using Vietnam as a case study context. These factors were identified through the lens of Contingency theory. By applying the sequential mixed method with three studies involving interviews, case studies, and a survey, the results of data analysis collected from the Study 1 were the inferences for the Study 2, which then generated the further implications for the Study 3. The answer of the overarching research problem comes from the synthesis of results from three studies. Seven factors finally emerged: (1) Top management; (2) Regional differences; (3) The intensity of market competition; (4) The support of business networks; (5) Organizational resources; (6) Organizational culture; and (7) Organizational strategy.

Top management

The role of top management has been discussed in much previous Balanced Scorecard focused research (Braam & Nijssen, 2008; Hendricks et al., 2004; Rogers, 1995; Tran, 2012). In particular, through the lens of Contingency theory, top management takes the main responsibility to select the relevant performance measurement approach to their business and to make sure the model operating effectively (Braam & Nijssen, 2008; Hambrick & Mason, 1984; Hendricks et al., 2004; Murphy & Southey, 2003).

This research once again confirms the role of top management in the successful adoption of the Balanced Scorecard in the Vietnamese SME context. In particular, this research stresses the qualifications and awareness of CEOs as well as their commitment as consistently the most influential factor in the Balanced Scorecard adoption. The age and gender of CEOs were also investigated for their impact on the extent of the Balanced Scorecard use in Vietnamese SMEs. In the structure of the management system in Vietnamese SMEs, the CEO is the most powerful and responsible person and controls the operations of the enterprises and its strategic goals, and development. The CEO's determination and involvement are essential to the success of the business operations.

Regional differences

In the three studies, regional differences were found to have a significant impact on the adoption of the Balanced Scorecard in Vietnamese SMEs. Over the last 50 years, Southern and Northern regions of Vietnam have experienced different social and political histories. They have led to "differences in motives, perceived success factors, and business problem" for entrepreneurs in the different areas (Benzing et al., 2005, p. 5). These differences influence how SMEs in different areas of Vietnam adopt and manage the Balanced Scorecard in their organization. Regional differences were occasionally mentioned in previous SME-focused research; however, the finding in this present research is new in its focus on the effect of unique historical circumstances on the adoption of the Balanced Scorecard in Vietnamese SMEs. This needs more research to examine whether regional differences should be added to the list of determinants of the Balanced Scorecard adoption among SMEs in different contexts.

The intensity of market competition

The intensity of market competition has been found in the literature as the main contingent factor that impacts the usage of Balanced Scorecard approach in organizations (Hoque & James, 2000; Maiga & Jacobs, 2003; Malmi, 2001). This present research reinforces previous research, especially with Contingency theory as its reference. The intense competitiveness of the sector powerfully affects the existence and growth of

SMEs. This further motivates SMEs to seek solutions to overcome this competitive pressure and achieve sustainable development. SMEs are stimulated to create a competitive advantage by differentiating themselves from their competitors. Successful Balanced Scorecard adoption is one of the best choices that Vietnamese SMEs could make to effectively implement a differential strategy.

The support of business networks

Normally, organizations in general and SMEs in particular are afraid of adopting innovative processes because they have no knowledge and experience. Huggins (2000) suggested that engaging in business networks is a good way for enterprises to survive. Networks can help organizations to reduce risks and improve access to business ideas, knowledge and capital (Kristiansen, 2004). The technical and experienced support of business networks would be very helpful for Vietnamese SMEs when adopting and implementing the Balanced Scorecard. This support can help the human and financial resources, and the time necessary to achieve success in business management. Instead of having to learn new models and application procedures by themselves, SMEs can receive a lot of support from the community. SMEs also avoid the failures of other enterprises and can design an appropriate plan for the adoption of the Balanced Scorecard. The more support they receive from the network and experienced people, the more confident they are to make the decision to adopt and implement the Balanced Scorecard.

Organizational resources

This research confirms the crucial role of organizational resources in the successful adoption of the Balanced Scorecard in Vietnamese SMEs. Previous research discovered that the implementation of the Balanced Scorecard in an organization requires well-prepared organizational resources for a long and complicated process (Andon et al., 2007; Lueg & Vu, 2015). Perera et al. (2007) found that lack of organizational resources is the main reason for not adopting the Balanced Scorecard. The findings of this research confirm that any company of any size can adopt the Balanced Scorecard depending on the level of organizational resources it prepared for its adoption. Implementation of the Balanced Scorecard requires endurance and thorough preparation in all of the perspectives of finance and human resources.

Organizational culture

Organizational culture is another factor that is confirmed by this research as impacting the successful adoption of the Balanced Scorecard in Vietnamese SMEs. For the CEO to make the decision on adopting and successfully implementing the Balanced Scorecard, Vietnamese SMEs need to build an organizational culture that focuses on centralized commitment, innovation, consensus and collaboration, and readiness to exchange ideas and take risks. Rogers (1995) suggested that centralized commitment can hinder decisions to innovate by being rigid and authoritarian. However, in the Vietnamese SME context, centralized commitment is necessary so that the CEO can focus his/her full power on directing and actively participating in the process of applying the Balanced Scorecard model until the implementation is complete. In addition to the direct and in-depth management of the SME, a CEO who is ready to innovate, is willing to share ideas and experience, and is ready to take risks, can accept the Balanced Scorecard for their performance management and achieve success.

Organizational strategy

Business strategy exerts a vital impact on the design, adoption, and diffusion of the innovation process (Chenhall, 2003; Fakhri, 2012; Garengo & Bititci, 2007; Hendricks et al., 2012; Liu et al., 2014). Although this research supports the impact of business strategy on the decision to adopt and the successful adoption of the Balanced Scorecard, it cannot confirm the impact of organizational strategy on the level of the Balanced Scorecard adoption in Vietnamese SMEs. This result can be explained by the finding that in the Vietnamese SMEs context, rather than by organizational strategy, the extent of the Balanced Scorecard adoption is decided by how good the preparation of organizational resources is, how innovative and collaborative the organizational culture is, how committed the CEO is, and how much support is received from the business networks. However, overall, organizational strategy still plays an important role in the successful adoption of the Balanced Scorecard in Vietnamese SMEs. The Balanced Scorecard was designed to help enterprises assess their activities, not just from the financial perspective of revenues, costs, and profits but also from other perspectives, in a balanced view. The Balanced Scorecard effectively addresses the shortcomings of short-term financial measures and reflects past performance by adding measures that are the driving forces for future business development. Therefore, a long-term organizational strategy that focuses on the quality of products and improvement of services, and on innovation for sustainable development, is appropriate for the successful adoption of the Balanced Scorecard in Vietnamese SMEs.

7.3. Contributions of this book

Theoretical contributions

This research extends previous studies of the Balanced Scorecard and factors determining its adoption in SMEs, especially in the special conditions of the transitional economy of Vietnam. Vietnam is a developing country with a unique economy (social-oriented market economy) that is manipulated by the market mechanism and regulated by the State, with various forms of ownership. It is debatable whether previous studies of Balanced Scorecard adoption in SMEs in developed countries are relevant to the SMEs in Vietnam with its specific characteristics. This present research has initiated a new research direction on the adoption of the Balanced Scorecard in SMEs in the context of transitional economies in general as well as in the context of the diversity of other economies.

By drawing on Contingency theory literature, the findings of this research raise implications for future Balanced Scorecard researchers. This research supports the use of the Contingency theory in the explorations of impact factors on the adoption of performance measurement systems in general and the Balanced Scorecard specifically. Contingency theory has been reviewed as a theory of management accounting and control since the 1970s (Otley, 2016). In 2003, Chenhall (2003) expressed support for the Contingency theory for the studying impact factors on the adoption of management accounting systems. Since then, Contingency theory has been used in theory-driven research on the impact of contingent variables on the adoption and implementation of performance measurement systems, including the Balanced Scorecard (Ahmad & Zabri, 2015; Cardoso Vieira Machado, 2013; Chenhall, 2003; Fakhri, 2012; Garengo & Bititci, 2007; Hendricks et al., 2012; Hoang et al., 2017; Hoque & James, 2000; Liu et al., 2014; Oghuvwu & Omoye, 2016; Quesado et al., 2014, 2016; Speckbacher et al., 2003; Zuriekat, 2005). Otley (2016) opined "Contingency theory has been one of the success stories of research in management accounting and control over the past forty years" (p. 55). This present research exemplifies the success of Contingency theory for future theory-driven research on the Balanced Scorecard and innovation adoption.

Based on the Contingency theory as the primary research theory, this research found seven factors affecting the successful adoption of the Balanced Scorecard in SMEs in Vietnam. They are *top management, regional differences, the intensity of market competition, organizational culture, organizational strategy, organizational resources,* and *the support of business networks*. Of these factors, regional differences and the support of business networks are new contingency variables related to the conditions of the Vietnamese transition economy. Although previous research supported the impact of regional differences and business networks on SMEs' development (Benzing et al., 2005; Berry et al., 2006; Clifton et al., 2010; Jordan, 2015; Major & Cordey-Hayes, 2000; Ralston et al., 1999; Zain & Ng, 2006), the relationship between these factors and the Balanced Scorecard adoption in SMEs is largely under-researched. This present research, therefore, makes a novel contribution to the relevant literature by adding these new factors to the list of determinants of the Balanced Scorecard adoption among SMEs. In addition, this research found that the size of firm, which was mentioned as a main contingency variable in previous Balanced Scorecard adoption studies, plays no role in the decision to adopt the Balanced Scorecard by Vietnamese SMEs. Rather, organizational resources are the new contingency factor that Vietnamese enterprises of any size need to consider when deciding to adopt the Balanced Scorecard. This finding contributes significantly to further research on the Balanced Scorecard in different sizes and in different socio-economic conditions.

Finally, this research contributes to the literature by using sequential mixed methods to explore the determinants of the adoption of the Balanced Scorecard in Vietnamese SMEs. Tashakkori et al. (1998) and Creswell et al. (2003) argued that within a complicated business environment, using the single methodological approaches cannot reveal the whole reality. Applying mixed methods in a combination of qualitative and quantitative approaches "provide a better understanding research problem than either approach alone" (Creswell & Plano Clark, 2007, p. 5). Previous relevant research was conducted using individual case studies or small surveys (Luu, 2010; Nguyen, 2017; Pham & Bui, 2015; Ta, 2019; Tran, 2012). Most of the previous research preferred to apply quantitative methods rather than using qualitative methods to organize the data collection and analysis. This led to the limitations in understanding human phenomena, especially the behaviour of SMEs' CEOs regarding their decision to adopt the Balanced Scorecard. For example, the responses of the participants would have been influenced by many factors, so the results could be not entirely objective, although on a standardized scale, this could be accounted for depending on the participants. By using mixed methods, this research exemplifies good practice by considering the phenomenon from multiple viewpoints, perspectives, positions, and standpoints. The exploratory qualitative studies in this present research assisted the quantitative study by identifying topics that are appropriate to the method of investigation. The quantitative study was then able to support the qualitative studies by generalizing the findings of a larger sample and by identifying groups that need in-depth study. The qualitative research also helped to explain the relationships among the variables found in the quantitative study. This encourages further research in the adoption of the Balanced Scorecard in the Vietnamese SME context to use the mixed methodologies to obtain good quality findings.

Managerial contributions

The Balanced Scorecard has been considered a good performance management model and is commonly applied all over the world in different kinds of enterprises. This has been proven by both literature and real business cases. However, under the conditions of the Vietnamese economy, to decide to adopt the Balanced Scorecard in SMEs, managers of companies need to consider the impact factors in advance. Applying the Balanced Scorecard or other innovations in SMEs is not a trend in Vietnam. To adopt such an innovation, enterprises need to consider their capacity and whether their present conditions meet the requirements of the Balanced Scorecard adoption. Vietnamese SMEs need to have long-term vision and willingness to invest in the future. All staff levels within a company from the top to the bottom need to understand the Balanced Scorecard. Careful consideration will ensure the feasibility of its adoption in their companies. The results of this present research provide information for the consideration of SMEs' executives in their decision to adopt the Balanced Scorecard.

Top management plays a very important role in promoting innovation in general and in accepting the Balanced Scorecard. The findings of this research emphasize the importance of leadership, especially of the CEOs, in the decision to adopt and in the success of the adoption of the Balanced Scorecard. This research focused on top management's qualifications and awareness of the Balanced Scorecard as well as their commitment to participate until the end to make sure the process is successful. The research findings show that the CEOs in Vietnamese SMEs play a decisive role in all business activities. If the CEO has a deep understand of the Balanced Scorecard, recognizes the benefits that this model brings not only as a value management system but also as an approach that connects managers and staffs closely, he/she can make the decision to apply and participate in implementation of this model until success. Top management in Vietnamese SMEs need to develop specific characteristics to successfully manage the adoption of the Balanced Scorecard in their company: I1) They need to become more involved in introducing performance monitoring throughout the company, (2) They need to understand that the use of indicators and criteria in the company's key processes is essential to the company's success, and (3) They must be well informed and support every attempt to improve the company's performance.

Thorough preparation of financial and human resources is also important for successful adoption of the Balanced Scorecard in Vietnamese SMEs: (1) Employees and staff must be knowledgeable about the Balanced Scorecard, (2) A good plan of financial resources is essential, and (3) Consultation with staff, specialists and experts on the Balanced Scorecard is important. Adoption of the Balanced Scorecard is a long-term process that requires much investment in consulting and training activities, and buying management software etc. The costs will vary depending on the company and the scale of operation, but they will arise in all parts of the organizations. The Balanced Scorecard is deployed throughout the system of a company, and relates to all members, and therefore, requires the staff to fully understand the theory and practice.

As a strategic interpretation tool, the Balanced Scorecard is built on a solid foundation of organizational strategy. However, many SMEs in general and Vietnamese SMEs in particular, have considerable limitations in their strategy that is based primarily on analysis of the previous year's results. When there is no clear business strategy, the implementation of the Balanced Scorecard will meet many difficulties in setting up a system of indicators and measures. On the other hand, the Balanced Scorecard enables SMEs to implement a flexible business strategy for maintaining their competitive advantage, making decisions about change and creating a dynamic business environment.

Organizational culture is another important supportive factor for the application of new management methods. In an SME with a strong culture, a new policy and new direction will be supported by all members, which will facilitate innovation and improvement of activities. Conversely, in an SME that does not focus on building culture, its activities will not comply with certain rules and standards, and the support and approval of all members will be difficult to gain. For the creation and development of enterprises, the construction and implementation of culture are very important. Without building a strong organizational culture, it is difficult to develop consensus for the long-term goals of the company, making it difficult to apply the Balanced Scorecard. This research findings suggest that the decision to adopt the Balanced Scorecard by Vietnamese SMEs is strongly impacted by an organizational culture of decentralization but, significantly, with the centralized commitment of CEOs to innovation, consensus and collaboration, readiness to take risks and to share ideas. A good organizational culture helps to make all members in the company feel more confident to apply a new system without being stressed and hesitant.

In addition to the effort from the business itself, the successful adoption of the Balanced Scorecard also requires the support of business networks. Experience sharing and technological support from Balanced Scorecard adopters can help SMEs planning to adopt the Balanced Scorecard to save time and money. From the business networks, SMEs can learn about the process of building and implementing the Balanced Scorecard, the difficulties that may arise, and the causes of failure of the project. They also have the chance to exchange practical experiences.

When the size of the businesses increases beyond the SME level, the demand for information also increases and strategies, activities and budgets must also change. SMEs that want to achieve sustainable development need to have vision, mission, and strategy that align with each other, for which the Balanced Scorecard is an appropriate tool. In theory, an organization has to consider four aspects when implementing the Balanced Scorecard (finance, customer, business process, and learning and growth). The organization then needs to build a measurement system and collect and analyze the data in the relationships between the four aspects. However, SMEs should not apply the Balanced Scorecard mechanically, but base it on the capacity and size of their business.

Government policy contributions

To promote the expansion of the adoption of the Balanced Scorecard in Vietnamese SMEs effectively, the SMEs need the support of the government through macro policies. Government support is an effective means of enhancing innovative performance, especially for startups and formal SMEs in Vietnam (Tran & Vu, 2018)

Firstly, the government needs to issue specific guidelines and policies to enhance awareness and understanding of SMEs about the Balanced Scorecard. In fact, many SMEs in Vietnam know very little or nothing at all about the Balanced Scorecard, despite the usefulness of this model having been evidenced all over the world and in all sizes of companies. The government should: (1) organize the teaching about the Balanced Scorecard in universities of economics; (2) promote research on the adoption and implementation of the Balanced Scorecard, especially in Vietnamese SMEs; (3) support conferences and seminars on this topic.

Secondly, the government needs to issue policies to support both material and professional knowledge in promotion of the expansion of the application of the Balanced Scorecard in SMEs. It is necessary to create a positive relationship between the government's assistance fund for technological development and the promotion of innovation and innovation activities of SMEs. In addition, the government needs to encourage SMEs that have successfully implemented this model to share their experiences with the others.

Further, the government needs to enact regulations that inspect, and monitor localities for the full and effective implementation of policies to support SMEs. Currently, many localities pay more attention to SMEs, but because of the regional differences, the implementation of policies to support SMEs in each locality is different, causing distortion in the economy, dispersal of resources and failure to achieve socio-development goals. The support for SMEs should be focused and given a definite time limit, not be scattered, or generalized. Priority should be given to the type of SME in each specific business area based on the SME's immediate and long-term goals. However, such support should be provided in terms of specific funding sources and resources to limit the imbalance of the national economy.

7.4. Limitations and Further research

This research has some limitations and contributions that need to be addressed in further research.

Size and regional balance of the sample is a limitation of this research. The respondents in Study 1 (semi-structure interview) were not evenly spread across the three regions. There were 14 interviewees from Southern provinces, but only 9 from Central provinces and 9 from Northern provinces. This may lead to research results being more influenced by the participants of Southern SMEs. Further research could focus on an equal number of interviewees from each region. In addition, the collection of more questionnaires in each region than this present research (Study 3) may discover more specific aspects of Balanced Scorecard adoption of SMEs in each area in Vietnam and enable more comparisons.

In the process of question preparation for the interviews, we asked for contributions from participants from the Balanced Scorecard adopter large companies. However, there were no interviews of representatives from large Balanced Scorecard adopting companies and Balanced Scorecard experts. Their opinions are valuable and can contribute toward drawing a comprehensive picture of the Balanced Scorecard adoption in Vietnamese SMEs. Further research could open the sample to both Balanced Scorecard adopting SMEs and large companies to achieve a full picture from different perspectives.

The first Balanced Scorecard was designed and applied to a large company in the United State, and the research on the adoption and implementation of the Balanced Scorecard into businesses was mainly conducted in Western and developed countries. Recently, the research on the Balanced Scorecard application has been conducted about SMEs. Asian countries and developing countries have also started investing in the application of the Balanced Scorecard as an effective performance measurement approach that is relevant for SMEs. However, the foundation for Balanced Scorecard studies in SMEs in developing countries is based on Balanced Scorecard studies in large enterprises in developed and Western countries. Following the trend, studies of the Balanced Scorecard in Vietnamese SMEs also use the theory of Balanced Scorecard in large enterprises as a conceptual framework. This present research is one of the first studies of the Balanced Scorecard in SMEs conducted throughout the whole of Vietnam. Because the field is under-researched, not much knowledge was available for this research given that most of the scales used were originally designed for the research on the Balanced Scorecard in large enterprises in Western and developed countries. This present research adjusted these scales to fit the business environment in Vietnam, which provides an appropriate set of scale for future studies on the Balanced Scorecard in Vietnamese SMEs.

The historical and socioeconomic differences between Southern and Northern regions of Vietnam require different ways of adopting of the Balanced Scorecard by SMEs in these areas. Fisher and Härtel (2004), and Avermaete et al. (2003) highlighted the importance of intracultural differences when examining business processes. Desiring to understand the impact of regional differences on the performance of Vietnamese enterprises, especially SMEs, has always attracted the attention of many researchers. The findings of this book provide the knowledge that can become the basis for further research on this variable. In addition, the present research also opens the opportunity for further study on the impact of culture on the Balanced Scorecard adoption in Vietnamese SMEs.

Networks have been considered as a good support for SMEs in their efforts to improve development. Networks can support SMEs to increase their capacity to access resources, technology, or information when considering innovation (Evans et al., 2017; Premaratne, 2001). This present research confirms the importance of the business network's role in the use of the Balanced Scorecard in Vietnamese SMEs. Thus, this research provides theoretical and practical groundwork for future research on the relationship between business networks and innovation approach in SME.

Top management has been much researched in studies of innovation application of businesses. This present research found that in Vietnamese SMEs, CEOs individually, rather than the whole top management board, are the most important persons in all of decision making in a company. Previous studies of the Balanced Scorecard adoption focused on analysing the impact of top management, but not specifically on the importance and influence of the CEO. This research opens opportunities for further research on the relationship between CEOs, Balanced Scorecard adoption and other innovations in Vietnamese SMEs.

7.5. Conclusion

This research is among the very first studies to investigate the Balanced Scorecard adoption in Vietnamese SMEs nationwide. This research provides several valuable insights into issues related to the Balanced Scorecard approach and SMEs' performance measurement systems. Contributions to theory in the general literature on the Balanced Scorecard implementation in SMEs as well as to the specific literature on Balanced Scorecard adoption by SMEs in developing countries are accompanied by useful theoretical and practical contributions to knowledge about adoption of the Balanced Scorecard by Vietnamese SMEs. This new knowledge will encourage the use of the Balanced Scorecard by SMEs for better operation. In addition, this new knowledge opens many opportunities for further research to explore Balanced Scorecard adoption in greater depth.

Bibliography

Abdel-Maksoud, A., Dugdale, D., & Luther, R. (2005). Non-financial performance measurement in manufacturing companies. *The British Accounting Review, 37*(3), 261-297.

Ahmad, K., & Zabri, M. (2015). Factors explaining the use of management accounting practices in Malaysian medium-sized firms. *Journal of Small Business and Enterprise Development, 22*(4), 762-781.

Al-Omiri, M. F. R. (2003). *The diffusion of management accounting innovations: a study of the factors influencing the adoption, implementation levels and success of ABC.* (Doctoral dissertation). University of Huddersfield)

Anand, M., Sahay, S., & Saha, S. (2005). Balanced Scorecard in Indian Companies. *Vikalpa, 30*(2), 11-26. doi:10.1177/0256090920050202

Andersen, H., Cobbold, I., & Lawrie, G. (2001). *Balanced scorecard implementation in SMEs: reflection on literature and practice.* Paper presented at the Proceedings of the Fourth SME International Conference, Aalborg University, Aalborg, Denmark.

Andon, P., Baxter, J., & Chua, W. F. (2007). Accounting change as relational drifting: A field study of experiments with performance measurement. *Management Accounting Research, 18*(2), 273-308.

Appiah-Adu, K., & Singh, S. (1998). Customer orientation and performance: a study of SMEs. *Management Decision, 36*(6), 385-394.

Aryani, Y. A., & Setiawan, D. (2020). Balanced Scorecard: Is it beneficial enough? A literature review. *Asian Journal of Accounting Perspectives, 13*(1), 65-84.

Ashurst, C., & Doherty, N. F. (2003). Towards the formulation of 'a best practice'framework for benefits realisation in IT projects. *Electronic Journal of Information Systems Evaluation, 6*(2), 1-10.

Asiaei, K., & Jusoh, R. (2014). Determinants of performance measurement practices: Toward a contingency framework. *International Journal of Management Excellence, 2*(3), 257-269.

Ates, A., Garengo, P., Cocca, P., & Bititci, U. (2013). The development of SME managerial practice for effective performance management. *Journal of Small Business and Enterprise Development, 20*(1), 28-54.

Atkinson, A. A., Balakrishnan, R., Booth, P., & Cote, J. M. (1997). New directions in management accounting research. *Journal of Management Accounting Research, 9*, 79-108.

Aurelia, S., Cardonib, A., Del Baldoc, M., & Lombardid, R. (2018). The balanced scorecard logic in the management control and reporting of small business company networks: A case study. *Accounting and Management Information Systems, 17*(2), 191-214.

Avermaete, T., Viaene, J., Morgan, E. J., & Crawford, N. (2003). Determinants of innovation in small food firms. *European Journal of Innovation Management, 6*(1), 8-17.

Awadallah, E. A., & Allam, A. (2015). A critique of the balanced scorecard as a performance measurement tool. *International Journal of Business and Social Science, 6*(7), 91-99.

Ax, C., & Bjørnenak, T. (2005). Bundling and diffusion of management accounting innovations—the case of the balanced scorecard in Sweden. *Management Accounting Research, 16*(1), 1-20.

Ayyagari, M., Beck, T., & Demirguc-Kunt, A. (2007). Small and medium enterprises across the globe. *Small Business Economics, 29*(4), 415-434.

Bach, T., Harvie, C., & Le, T. (2021a). How credit constraints affect small and medium enterprises' strategic employment decisions and employees' labour outcomes: evidence from recent credit crunch in Vietnam. *The Economics of Transition and Institutional Change,* 29(2), 319-341.

Bach, T., Le, T., & Bui, Y. (2021b). Informal short-term borrowings and firms' performance in a credit crunch: evidence from Vietnam. *Journal of Development Studies*, 57(8), 1321-1335.

Bach, T., Le, T., Hoang, K., & Nguyen, T. (2023). Gender discrimination, social networks and access to informal finance of Vietnamese small and medium enterprises. *Economic Analysis and Policy,* forthcoming.

Baird, K. M., Harrison, G., & Reeve, R. (2007). Success of activity management practices: the influence of organizational and cultural factors. *Accounting & Finance, 47*(1), 47-67.

Baird, K. M., Harrison, G. L., & Reeve, R. C. (2004). Adoption of activity management practices: A note on the extent of adoption and the influence of organizational and cultural factors. *Management Accounting Research, 15*(4), 383-399.

Barker, T., & Üngör, M. (2019). Vietnam: The Next Asian Tiger? *The North American Journal of Economics and Finance, 47*, 96-118.

Basuony, M. A. (2014). The Balanced Scorecard in large firms and SMEs: A critique of the nature, value and application. *Accounting and Finance*

Research, 3(2), 14-22.

Benzing, C., Chu, H. M., & Callanan, G. (2005). A regional comparison of the motivation and problems of Vietnamese entrepreneurs. *Journal of Developmental Entrepreneurship, 10*(01), 3-27.

Beresford, M. (2008). Doi Moi in review: The challenges of building market socialism in Vietnam. *Journal of Contemporary Asia, 38*(2), 221-243.

Berry, A. J., Sweeting, R., & Goto, J. (2006). The effect of business advisers on the performance of SMEs. *Journal of Small Business and Enterprise Development, 13*(1), 33-47.

Bertolini, P., & Giovannetti, E. (2006). Industrial districts and internationalization: The case of the agri-food industry in Modena, Italy. *Entrepreneurship and Regional Development, 18*(4), 279-304.

Bigsten, A., & Söderbom, M. (2006). What have we learned from a decade of manufacturing enterprise surveys in Africa? *The World Bank Research Observer, 21*(2), 241-265.

Birch, C. (1998). Balanced scorecard points to wins for small firms. *AUSTRALIAN CPA, 68*, 43-45.

Bisbe, J., & Barrubés, J. (2012). The Balanced Scorecard as a management tool for assessing and monitoring strategy implementation in health care organizations. *Revista Española de Cardiología (English Edition), 65*(10), 919-927.

Bititci, U. S. (1994). Measuring your way to profit. *Management Decision, 32*(6), 16-24.

Bititci, U. S., Garengo, P., Dörfler, V., & Nudurupati, S. (2012). Performance measurement: challenges for tomorrow. *International journal of management reviews, 14*(3), 305-327.

Bititci, U. S., Nudurupati, S. S., Turner, T. J., & Creighton, S. (2002). Web Enabled Performance Measurement Systems - Management Implications. *International Journal of Operations & Production Management, 22*(11), 1273 - 1287.

Bititci, U. S., Turner, U. T., & Begemann, C. (2000). Dynamics of performance measurement systems. *International Journal of Operations & Production Management, 20*(6), 692-704.

Blackburn, R. A., Hart, M., & Wainwright, T. (2013). Small business performance: Business, strategy and owner-manager characteristics. *Journal of Small Business and Enterprise Development*, 8-22.

Bose, S., & Thomas, K. (2007). Applying the balanced scorecard for better performance of intellectual capital. *Journal of Intellectual Capital, 8*(4), 653-665.

Bourgeois, L. J. (1980). Strategy and environment: A conceptual integration. *Academy of Management Review, 5*(1), 25-39.

Bourne, M. (2008). Performance measurement: Learning from the past and projecting the future. *Measuring Business Excellence, 12*(4), 67-72.

Braam, G. J. M., & Nijssen, E. J. (2008). Exploring the antecedents of Balanced Scorecard adoption as a performance measurement and strategic management system. *NiCE Working Paper 08-115 December 2008*.

Brignall, T. J., Fitzgerald, L., Johnston, R., & Silvestro, R. (1991). Performance measurement in service businesses. *Management Accounting, 69*(10), 34-36.

Brislin, R. W. (1970). Back-translation for cross-cultural research. *Journal of cross-cultural psychology, 1*(3), 185-216.

Brislin, R. W., Lonner, W., & Thorndike, R. (1973). *Cross-cultural methods*. New York: John Wiley and Sons, .

Bruns, W. J., & Waterhouse, J. H. (1975). Budgetary control and organization structure. *Journal of Accounting Research*, 177-203.

Bryman, A., & Bell, E. (2001). The nature of qualitative research. *Social Research Methods*, 365-399.

Bui, T. H. V. (2009). *Factors affect to plan of Balanced scorecard application in Vietnamese small and medium enterprises.* (Master) Ho Chi Minh City University of Technology.

Burns, T. E., & Stalker, G. M. (1961). *The management of innovation*: Oxford University Press.

Butler, A., Letza, S. R., & Neale, B. (1997). Linking the balanced scorecard to strategy. *Long Range Planning, 30*(2), 242153-242253.

Cadez, S., & Guilding, C. (2008). An exploratory investigation of an integrated contingency model of strategic management accounting. *Accounting, Organizations and Society, 33*(7), 836-863.

Calza, E., Goedhuys, M., & Trifković, N. (2019). Drivers of productivity in Vietnamese SMEs: The role of management standards and innovation. *Economics of Innovation and New Technology, 28*(1), 23-44.

Can, V. L. (2017). *SMEs development: Vietnamese Experiences*. Paper presented at the APEC's post 2020 Agenda: Rising Protectionism, Economic Rebalancing, and Diversified Growth Conference, Songapore.

Carbonara, E., Tran, H. T., & Santarelli, E. (2019). Determinants of novice, portfolio, and serial entrepreneurship: an occupational choice approach. *Small Business Economics*, 1-29.

Cardoso Vieira Machado, M. J. (2013). Balanced Scorecard: an empirical study of small and medium size enterprises. *Revista Brasileira de Gestão de Negócios, 15*(46), 129-148.

Čater, T., & Pučko, D. (2010). Factors of effective strategy implementation: Empirical evidence from Slovenian business practice. *Journal for East European Management Studies*, 207-236.

Cengic, M., & Fazlic, D. (2008). *Balanced Scorecard vs. Performance Prism.* Paper presented at the 12th International Research/Expert Conference "Trends in the Development of Machinery and Associated Technology, Istanbul.

Challis, D., Samson, D., & Lawson, B. (2005). Impact of technological, organizational and human resource investments on employee and manufacturing performance: Australian and New Zealand evidence. *International Journal of Production Research, 43*(1), 81-107.

Chan, Y. C. L. (2004). Performance measurement and adoption of balanced scorecards: A survey of municipal governments in the USA and Canada. *International Journal of Public Sector Management, 17*, 204-221.

Chavan, M. (2009). The balanced scorecard: A new challenge. *Journal of Management Development, 28*(5), 393-406.

Chell, E., & Baines, S. (1998). Does gender affect business "oerformance"? A study of microbusinesses in the UK. *Entrepreneurshup & Regional Development, An International Journal., 10*(2), 117-135.

Chen, H., Duh, R.-R., & Lin, J. C.-C. (2006). The determinants of implementation stages of balanced scorecard. *International Journal of Management and Decision Making, 7*(4), 356-376.

Chen, H., & Miao, Y. (2010). *Knowledge Management for SMEs Based on the Balanced Scorecard.* Paper presented at the International Conference on Management and Service Science (MASS), Wuhan, China.

Cheng, M. M., & Humphreys, K. A. (2012). The differential improvement effects of the strategy map and scorecard perspectives on managers' strategic judgments. *The Accounting Review, 87*(3), 899-924.

Chenhall, R. H. (2003). Management control systems design within its organizational context: findings from contingency-based research and directions for the future. *Accounting, Organizations and Society, 28*(2), 127-168.

Chenhall, R. H., & Langfield-Smith, K. (1998). Adoption and benefits of management accounting practices: an Australian study. *Management Accounting Research, 9*(1), 1-19.

Chenhall, R. H., & Morris, D. (1986). The impact of structure, environment, and interdependence on the perceived usefulness of management accounting systems. *Accounting Review, 61*(1), 16-35.

Chia, Y. M., & Koh, H. C. (2007). Organizational culture and the adoption of management accounting practices in the public sector: A Singapore study. *Financial Accountability & Management, 23*(2), 189-213.

Chimwani, P. M., Nyamwange, O., & Otuyo, R. (2013). Application of strategic performance measures in Small and Medium-Sized Manufacturing Enterprises in Kenya: The use of the Balanced Scorecard perspectives. *International Journal of Management Sciences and Business Research, 2*(6).

Chiu, M. C., & Li, E. Y. (2014). *Investigating the Academic Trend of Balanced Scorecard from Bibliometric Approach.* Paper presented at the Computer, Consumer and Control (IS3C), 2014 International Symposium on.

Chong, H. G. (2008). Measuring performance of small-and-medium sized enterprises: The grounded theory approach. *Journal of Business and Public Affairs, 2*(1), 1-10.

Chong, P., Ong, T., Abdullah, A., & Choo, W. (2019). Internationalisation and innovation on balanced scorecard (BSC) among Malaysian small and medium enterprises (SMEs). *Management Science Letters, 9*(10), 1617-1632.

Chow, C. W., Haddad, K. M., & Williamson, J. E. (1997). Applying the balanced scorecard to small companies. *Strategic Finance, 79*(2), 21-27.

CIEM. (2016). *Characteristics of the Vietnamese business environment: Evidence from a survey in 2015.* Retrieved from Vietnam: https://www.wider.unu.edu/sites/default/files/SME2015-report-English.pdf

Clifton, N., Keast, R., Pickernell, D., & Senior, M. (2010). Network structure, knowledge governance, and firm performance: Evidence from innovation networks and SMEs in the UK. *Growth and Change, 41*(3), 337-373.

Cocca, P., & Alberti, M. (2010). A framework to assess performance measurement systems in SMEs. *International Journal of Productivity and Performance Management, 59*(2), 186-200.

Colclough, S. N., Moen, Ø., Hovd, N. S., & Chan, A. (2019). SME innovation orientation: Evidence from Norwegian exporting SMEs. *International Small Business Journal, 37*(8), 780-803.

Comrey, A. L., Backer, T. E., & Glaser, E. M. (1973). *A sourcebook for mental health measures*. Los Angeles: Human Interaction Research Institute.

Cooksey, R. W., & McDonald, G. (2011). *Writing up your research: Surviving and thriving in postgraduate research*: Tilde University Press.

Cooper, D. J., Ezzamel, M., & Qu, S. Q. (2017). Popularizing a management accounting idea: The case of the balanced scorecard. *Contemporary Accounting Research, 34*(2), 991-1025.

Cooper, D. J., & Schindler, P. (2001). *Business research methods* Boston: McGraw-Hill.

Corvellec, H. (2018). *Stories of achievements: Narrative features of organizational performance*: Routledge.

Creamer, G., & Freund, Y. (2010). Learning a board Balanced Scorecard to improve corporate performance. *Decision Support Systems, 49*(4), 365-385.

Cresswell, J. W. (2014). Research design: Qualitative, quantitative, and mixed methods approaches. In. New Jersey: Pearson Education.

Creswell, J. W. (1998). *Quality inquiry and research design: Choosing among five traditions*. Thousand Oaks: Sage.

Creswell, J. W. (2013). *Research design: Qualitative, quantitative, and mixed methods approaches*: Sage publications.

Creswell, J. W., Hanson, E., Plano Clark, V. L., & Morales, A. (2007). Qualitative research designs: Selection and implementation. *The Counseling Psychologist, 35*(2), 236-264.

Creswell, J. W., & Plano Clark, V. L. (2007). Designing and conducting mixed methods research In: Sage.

Creswell, J. W., & Plano Clark, V. L. (2011). Choosing a mixed methods design. In J. W. Creswell & V. L. Plano Clark (Eds.), *Designing design and conducting mixed methodsapproaches* (Vol. 2, pp. 53-106).

Creswell, J. W., & Plano Clark, V. L. (2011). Research design and conducting mixed method approaches. In. Thousand Oaks, CA: Sage

Creswell, J. W., Plano Clark, V. L., & Garrett, A. L. (2003). Advanced mixed methods research. In J. W. Creswell & V. L. Plano Clark (Eds.), *Handbook of mixed methods in social and behavioural research.* (pp. 209-240). Thousand

Oaks, CA: Sage.

Crotty, M. (1998). *The foundations of social research: Meaning and perspective in the research process*: Sage.

da Costa Marques, M. d. C. (2012). Strategic Management and Balanced Scorecard: The Particular Case of Small and Medium Enterprises (SMEs) In Portugal. *Business and Management Review, 2*(1), 50-62.

Danneels, E. (2002). The dynamics of product innovation and firm competences. *Strategic management journal, 23*(12), 1095-1121.

Darnall, N., & Edwards Jr, D. (2006). Predicting the cost of environmental management system adoption: the role of capabilities, resources and ownership structure. *Strategic management journal, 27*(4), 301-320.

Davig, W., Elbert, N., & Brown, S. (2004). Implementing a strategic planning model for small manufacturing firms: an adaptation of the balanced scorecard. *SAM Advanced Management Journal, 69*(1), 18-25.

De Geuser, F., Mooraj, S., & Oyon, D. (2009). Does the balanced scorecard add value? Empirical evidence on its effect on performance. *European Accounting Review, 18*(1), 93-122.

De Haas, M., & Kleingeld, A. (1999). Multilevel design of performance measurement systems: enhancing strategic dialogue throughout the organization. *Management Accounting Research, 10*(3), 233-261.

De Toni, A., & Tonchia, S. (2001). Performance measurement systems-models, characteristics and measures. *International journal of operations & production management, 21*(1/2), 46-71.

De Waal, A. A. (2003). The future of the balanced scorecard: an interview with Professor Dr Robert S. Kaplan. *Measuring Business Excellence, 7*(1), 30-35.

Denscombe, M. (2008). Communities of practice: A research paradigm for the mixed methods approach. *Journal of mixed methods research, 2*(3), 270-283.

Denton, D. K. (2005). Measuring relevant things. *International Journal of Productivity and Performance Management, 54*(4), 278-287.

Dinh, H. N., Tran, M. D., & Nguy, T. H. (2018). Determinants Influencing the Usage of Balanced Scorecard for Performance Measurement: The Case of Vietnam. *Academy of Accounting and Financial Studies Journal, 22*(6), 1-15.

Doan, N. P. A. (2012). *The Adoption of Western Management Accounting Prac-*

tices in Vietnamese Enterprises During Economic Transition. (PhD). Griffith University,

Doan, N. P. A., Nguyen, D.-T., & Mia, L. (2011). Western management accounting practices in Vietnamese enterprises: Adoption and perceived benefits. *Pacific Accounting Review, 23*(2), 142-164.

Eccles, R. (1991). The performance measurennent manifesto. *Harvard Business Review, January-February, 69*(1), 131-137.

Edwards, V., & Phan, A. (2013). *Managers and management in Vietnam: 25 years of economic renovation (Doi moi)* (Vol. 114): Routledge.

Eremenco, S. L., Cella, D., & Arnold, B. J. (2005). A comprehensive method for the translation and cross-cultural validation of health status questionnaires. *Evaluation & the health professions, 28*(2), 212-232.

Eurocham. (2011). *Tools for assessing business associations' capacity using modern criteria - Strengthening strategy and management capacity of business association.* Retrieved from Vietnam.

Evans, S., Vladimirova, D., Holgado, M., Van Fossen, K., Yang, M., Silva, E. A., & Barlow, C. Y. (2017). Business model innovation for sustainability: Towards a unified perspective for creation of sustainable business models. *Business Strategy and the Environment, 26*(5), 597-608.

Ewing, P., & Lundahl, L. (1996). *The balanced scorecard at ABB Sweden–the EVITA project.* Paper presented at the The International Workshop on Cost Management.

Fakhri, G. (2012). The Impact of Contingent Factors on the Use of Performance Measurement System in the Banking Industry in Developing Countries. *Journal of Performance Management, 24*(2), 45-70.

Falle, S., Rauter, R., Engert, S., & Baumgartner, R. J. (2016). Sustainability management with the sustainability balanced scorecard in SMEs: Findings from an Austrian case study. *Sustainability, 8*(6), 545-560.

Feilzer, Y. M. (2010). Doing mixed methods research pragmatically: Implications for the rediscovery of pragmatism as a research paradigm. *Journal of mixed methods research, 4*(1), 6-16.

Fernandes, K. J., Raja, V., & Whalley, A. (2006). Lessons from implementing the balanced scorecard in a small and medium size manufacturing organization. *Technovation, 26*(5-6), 623-634.

Field, A. (2013). *Discovering statistics using IBM SPSS statistics*: sage.

Field, T. (2000). *Touch therapy*: Elsevier Health Sciences.

Fisher, G. B., & Härtel, C. E. (2004). Evidence for crossvergence in the perception of task and contextual performance: a study of Western expatriates working in Thailand. *Cross Cultural Management: An International Journal, 11*(2), 3-15.

Folan, P., & Browne, J. (2005). A review of performance measurement: Towards performance management. *Computers in industry, 56*(7), 663-680.

Garengo, P., & Biazzo, S. (2012). Unveiling strategy in SMEs through balanced scorecard implementation: A circular methodology. *Total Quality Management & Business Excellence, 23*(1), 79-102.

Garengo, P., Biazzo, S., & Bititci, U. (2005). Performance Measurement Systems in SMEs: A Review for a Research Agenda. *International Journal of Management Review*, 7(1), 25-47.

Garengo, P., & Bititci, U. (2007). Towards a contingency approach to performance measurement: an empirical study in Scottish SMEs. *International Journal of Operations & Production Management, 27*(8), 802-825.

Garver, M. S., & Mentzer, J. T. (1999). Logistics research methods: employing structural equation modeling to test for construct validity. *Journal of business logistics, 20*(1), 33-57.

George, D., & Mallery, M. (2010). SPSS for Windows Step by Step: A Simple Guide and Reference 17.0 Update Pearson. *Boston, MA*.

Ghasemi, A., & Zahediasl, S. (2012). Normality tests for statistical analysis: a guide for non-statisticians. *International journal of endocrinology and metabolism, 10*(2), 486-489.

Giannopoulos, G., Holt, A., Khansalar, E., & Cleanthous, S. (2013). The use of the Balanced Scorecard in small companies. *International Journal of Business and Management, 8*(14), 1-22.

Glaser, L., Fourne, S. P., & Elfring, T. (2015). Achieving strategic renewal: The multi-level influences of top and middle managers' boundary-spanning. *Small Business Economics, 45*(2), 305-327.

Gosselin, M. (1997). The effect of strategy and organizational structure on the adoption and implementation of activity-based costing. *Accounting, organizations and society, 22*(2), 105-122.

Government of Vietnam. (1988). *Directive 81-CT issued 24 March 1988 on the implementation of the Council of Ministers Decree 27&28-HDBT*. Hanoi, Vietnam

Greener, S. (2008). *Business research methods*: BookBoon.

Grigoroudis, E., Orfanoudaki, E., & Zopounidis, C. (2012). Strategic performance measurement in a healthcare organisation: A multiple criteria approach based on balanced scorecard. *Omega, 40*(1), 104-119.

Guba, E. G., & Lincoln, Y. S. (1994). Competing paradigms in qualitative research. *Handbook of qualitative research,* 2(163-194), 105.

Guba, E. G., & Lincoln, Y. S. (2004). Competing paradigms in qualitative research: Theories and issues. *Approaches to qualitative research: A reader on theory and practice*, 17-38.

Gunasekaran, A., Marri, H. B., & Grieve, R. J. (1999). Activity based costing in small and medium enterprises. *Computers & Industrial Engineering, 37*(1-2), 407-411.

Gunawan, G., Ellis-Chadwick, F., & King, M. (2008). An empirical study of the uptake of performance measurement by Internet retailers. *Internet Research, 18*, 361 - 381.

Hair, J. F., Black, W. C., Babin, B. J., & Anderson, R. E. (2019). *Multivariate data analysis*: Hampshire, UK: Cengage Learning, EMEA.

Hair, J. F., Black, W. C., Babin, B. J., Anderson, R. E., & Tatham, R. L. (1998). *Multivariate data analysis* (Vol. 5): Prentice hall Upper Saddle River, NJ.

Hair, J. F., Black, W. C., Babin, B. J., Anderson, R. E., & Tatham, R. L. (2009). *Análise multivariada de dados*: Bookman Editora.

Hambrick, D. C., & Mason, P. A. (1984). Upper echelons: The organization as a reflection of its top managers. *Academy of management review, 9*(2), 193-206.

Hanif, A., & Manarvi, I. A. (2010). *Investigating the implementation of balanced scorecard in Pakistani small enterprises.* Paper presented at the Advanced Management Science (ICAMS), 2010 IEEE International Conference (Vol 2), 574-578.

Hansen, H., Rand, J., & Tarp, F. (2009). Enterprise growth and survival in Vietnam: does government support matter? *The Journal of Development Studies, 45*(7), 1048-1069.

Harvie, C. (2001). Competition policy and SMEs in Vietnam.

Harvie, C. (2004). The contribution of SMEs in the economic transition of Vietnam. *Journal for International Business and Entrepreneurship Development,* 2(2), 1-16.

Hasan, R. U., & Chyi, T. M. (2017). Practical Application of Balanced Scorecard-A Literature Review. *Journal of Strategy and Performance Management, 5*(3), 87-103.

Hatry, H. P. (2006). *Performance measurement: Getting results*: The Urban Insitute.

Hax, A. C., & Majluf, N. S. (1984). Strategic management: an integrative perspective.

Heckl, D., & Moormann, J. (2010). Process performance management. In *Handbook on business process management 2* (pp. 115-135): Springer.

Heinicke, A. (2018). Performance measurement systems in small and medium-sized enterprises and family firms: a systematic literature review. *Journal of Management Control, 28*(4), 457-502.

Hendricks, K., Hora, M., Menor, L., & Wiedman, C. (2012). Adoption of the balanced scorecard: A contingency variables analysis. *Canadian Journal of Administrative Sciences/Revue Canadienne des Sciences de l'Administration, 29*(2), 124-138.

Hendricks, K., Menor, L., & Wiedman, C. (2004). The Balanced Scorecard: To adopt or not to adopt. *Ivey Business Journal, 69*(2), 1-7.

Henri, J.-F. (2006). Management control systems and strategy: A resource-based perspective. *Accounting, organizations and society, 31*(6), 529-558.

Henschel, T. (2006). Risk management practices in German SMEs: an empirical investigation. *International Journal of Entrepreneurship and Small Business, 3*(5), 554-571.

Hoang, V. T., Dinh, H. N., & Nhuy, T. H. (2017). *Factors influencing the usage of balanced scorecard for performance measurement in enterprises in Vietnam.* Paper presented at the For Young Researchers in Economics and Business, 2017, Hanoi.

Hoe, S. L. (2008). Issues and procedures in adopting structural equation modeling technique. *Journal of Applied Quantitative Methods, 3*(1), 76-83.

Hoelter, J. W. (1983). The analysis of covariance structures: Goodness-of-fit indices. *Sociological Methods & Research, 11*(3), 325-344.

Hoque, Z. (2004). A contingency model of the association between strategy, environmental uncertainty and performance measurement: impact on organizational performance. *International Business Review, 13*(4), 485-502.

Hoque, Z. (2014). 20 years of studies on the balanced scorecard: Trends, accomplishments, gaps and opportunities for future research. *The British Accounting Review, 46*(1), 33-59.

Hoque, Z., & James, W. (2000). Linking balanced scorecard measures to size and market factors: impact on organizational performance. *Journal of management accounting research, 12*(1), 1-17.

Hourneaux Jr, F., Carneiro-da-Cunha, J. A., & Corrêa, H. L. (2017). Performance measurement and management systems. *Managerial Auditing Journal, 32*(2), 148-166.

Huber, E., Ragin, C., & Stephens, J. D. (1993). Social democracy, Christian democracy, constitutional structure, and the welfare state. *American Journal of Sociology, 99*(3), 711-749.

Hudson, M., Lean, J., & Smart, A. (2001). Improving control through effective performance measurement in SMEs. *Production Planning & Control, 12*(8), 804-813.

Hudson, M., Smart, A., & Bourne, M. (2001). Theory and practise in SME performance measurement systems. *International journal of Operations and Production Management, 21*(8), 1096-1115.

Huggins, R. (2000). The success and failure of policy-implanted inter-firm network initiatives: motivations, processes and structure. *Entrepreneurship & Regional Development, 12*(2), 111-135.

Hussin, A., & Yusoff, R. Z. B. (2013). Adapting the BSC for SMEs–observations from an action research study. *Management, 3*(7), 448-458.

Hvolby, H.-H., & Thorstenson, A. (2001). Indicators for performance measurement in small and medium-sized enterprises. *Proceedings of the Institution of Mechanical Engineers, Part B: Journal of Engineering Manufacture, 215*(8), 1143-1146.

Inamdar, N., Kaplan, R. S., & Reynolds, K. (2002). Applying the balanced scorecard in healthcare provider organizations/Practitioner's Response. *Journal of Healthcare Management, 47*(3), 179-195.

Islam, J., & Hu, H. (2012). A review of literature on contingency theory in managerial accounting. *African Journal of Business Management, 6*(15), 5159-5164.

Ittner, C. D., & Larcker, D. F. (2001). Assessing empirical research in managerial accounting: a value-based management perspective. *Journal of accounting and economics, 32*(1-3), 349-410.

Jabeen, F., & Behery, M. (2017). Exploring the status and effects of balanced scorecard adoption in the non-western context: Evidence from the Middle East. *Journal of Management Development, 36*(8), 1063-1075.

Jensen, M. C., & Meckling, W. (1976). Theory of the firm: Managerial behavior, agency costs and ownership structure. *Journal of Financial Economics, 3*(4).

Johanson, U., Skoog, M., Backlund, A., & Almqvist, R. (2006). Balancing dilemmas of the balanced scorecard. *Accounting, Auditing & Accountability Journal, 19*(6), 842-857.

Johnson, H. T. (2013). *A New Approach to Management Accounting History (RLE Accounting)*: Routledge.

Johnson, R. B., Onwuegbuzie, A. J., & Turner, L. A. (2007). Toward a definition of mixed methods research. *Journal of Mixed Methods Research, 1*(2), 112-133.

Jordan, D. (2015). Location and business-level product innovation in Vietnam: Regional differences and drivers. *The Australasian Journal of Regional Studies, 21*(2), 232.

Juhmani, O. (2007). Usage, motives and usefulness of the Balanced Scorecard: Evidence from Bahrain. *International Journal of Business Research, 7*(5), 106-117.

Kaplan, R.S., & Bruns, W.J. (1987). Accounting and Management: Field study perspectives.

Kaplan, R. S. (2001). Strategic performance measurement and management in nonprofit organizations. *Nonprofit Management and Leadership, 11*(3), 353-370.

Kaplan, R. S. (2009). Conceptual foundations of the balanced scorecard. In C. S. Chapman, A. G. Hopwood, & M. D. Shields (Eds.), *Handbook of management accounting research* (Vol. 3), 1253-1269.

Kaplan, R. S., & Norton, D. P. (1992). The Balanced Scorecard – Measures that drive performance. *Harvard Business Review, 70*(1), 11.

Kaplan, R. S., & Norton, D. P. (1996). *The Balanced Scorecard: Translating strategy into action*: Harvard Business Press.

Kaplan, R. S., & Norton, D. P. (1996). Strategic learning & the Balanced Scorecard. *Strategy & Leadership, 24*(5), 18-24.

Kaplan, R.S., & Norton,D.P. (1996). Using the balanced scorecard as a strategic management system. In: Harvard business review Boston.

Kaplan, R.S., & Norton,D.P. (1996). Using the balanced scorecard as a strategic management system. In: Harvard business review Boston.

Kaplan, R. S., & Norton, D. P. (2001). The strategy-focused organization. *Strategy and Leadership, 29*(3), 41-42.

Kaplan, R. S., & Norton, D. P. (2004). Measuring the strategic readiness of intangible assets. *Harvard Business Review, 82*(2), 52-63.

Kaplan, R. S., & Norton, D. P. (2008). *The execution premium: Linking strategy to operations for competitive advantage*: Harvard Business Press.

Kaplan, R. S., & Norton, D. P. (2008). Mastering the management system. *Harvard Business Review, 86*(1), 62.

Kasiri, N., Sharda, R., & Hardgrave, B. (2012). A balanced scorecard for item-level RFID in the retail sector: a Delphi study. *European Journal of Information Systems, 21*(3), 255-267.

Kasperskaya, Y. (2008). Implementing the balanced scorecard: a comparative study of two Spanish city councils–an institutional perspective. *Financial Accountability & Management, 24*(4), 363-384.

Kasurinen, T. (2002). Exploring management accounting change: the case of balanced scorecard implementation. *Management Accounting Research, 13*(3), 323-343.

Kennerley, M., Neely, A., & Adams, C. (2003). Survival of the fittest: measuring performance in a changing business environment. *Measuring Business Excellence, 7*(4), 37-43.

Killam, L. (2013). *Research terminology simplified: Paradigms, axiology, ontology, epistemology and methodology*: Laura Killam.

Kim, J., & Rhee, J. (2012). An empirical study on the impact of critical success factors on the balanced scorecard performance in Korean green supply chain management enterprises. *International Journal of Production Research, 50*(9), 2465-2483.

Kim, Y., & Kang, M. (2016). The Performance Management System of the Korean healthcare sector: development, challenges, and future tasks. *Public Performance & Management Review, 39*(2), 297-315.

King, N. (2004). Using templates in the thematic analysis of text. *Essential guide to qualitative methods in organizational research, 2*, 256-270.

King, N. (2012). Doing template analysis. *Qualitative organizational research: Core methods and current challenges, 426*.

Kivunja, C., & Kuyini, A. B. (2017). Understanding and applying research paradigms in educational contexts. *International Journal of Higher Education, 6*(5), 26-41.

Klapper, L., Laeven, L., & Rajan, R. (2004). *Business environment and firm entry: Evidence from international data*. The World Bank.

Kokko, A., & Tingvall, P. G. (2005). *Regional development and government support to SMEs in Vietnam*: Sida, Department for Policy and Methodology.

Koske, C., & Muturi, W. (2015). Factors affecting the application of balanced score card: A case study of nongovernmental organisations in Eldoret, Kenya. *The Strategic Journal of Business Management and Change, 2*(2), 1868-1898.

Koufteros, X., Vonderembse, M., & Jayaram, J. (2005). Internal and external integration for product development: the contingency effects of uncertainty, equivocality, and platform strategy. *Decision Sciences, 36*(1), 97-133.

Kristiansen, S. (2004). Social networks and business success: The role of subcultures in an African context. *American Journal of Economics and Sociology, 63*(5), 1149-1171.

Kueng, P., Meier, A., Wettstein, T., & Meier, A. (2000). *Computer-based performance measurement in SMEs: is there any option?* : Institute of Informatics-University of Fribourg.

Kuhn, T. S. (1962). *The structure of scientific revolutions* (Vol. 2): The University of Chicago Press.

Kuhn, T. S. (1970). *Criticism and the growth of knowledge: Volume 4: Proceedings of the International Colloquium in the Philosophy of Science, London, 1965* (Vol. 4): Cambridge University Press.

Kumar, N. (2001). *Organizational Behavior*. New Delhi: : Anmol publications limited.

Kumru, M. (2012). A balanced scorecard-based composite measuring approach to assessing the performance of a media outlet. *The Service Industries Journal, 32*(5), 821-843.

Kureshi, N. (2014). To balanced scorecard or not to balanced scorecard, That is the question. *Journal of Strategy and Performance Management, 2*(1), 31-38.

Kureshi, N., Mann, R., Khan, M., & Qureshi, M. (2009). Quality management practices of SMEs in developing countries: A Ssurvey of manufacturing SMEs in Pakistan. *Journal of Quality and Technology Management, 5*(2), 63-89.

Kurtzman, J. (1997). Is your company off course? Now you can find out why. *Time & Life*.

Laitinen, E. K. (2002). A dynamic performance measurement system: evidence from small Finnish technology companies. *Scandinavian Journal of Management, 18*(1), 65-99.

Länsiluoto, A., Joensuu-Salo, S., Varamäki, E., Viljamaa, A., & Sorama, K. (2018). Market orientation and performance measurement system adoption impact on performance in SMEs. *Journal of Small Business Management*.

Lather, P. (1986). Research as praxis. *Harvard Educational Review, 56*(3), 257-278.

Lawrence, P., & Lorch, J. (1967). Organization and Environment, Graduate School of Business Administration, Harvard University. *Boston, MASS, USA*.

Le, M. D. (2017). ERP and Application Status: A Review of Vietnam's SMEs. *Journal of Research in Business, Economics and Management, 8*(6), 1577-1587.

Le, V., & Harvie, C. (2010). Firm performance in Vietnam: Evidence from manufacturing small and medium enterprises: workiing paper 04-10. In. Wollongong: University of Wollongong.

Le, X. S. (1997). Developing SMEs in transition economy: The case of Vietnam. (Ph. D Book). *Moscow National University, Russian Federation, Moscow*.

Lee, S.-H., Wong, P.-K., & Chong, C.-L. (2005). Human and social capital explanations for R&D outcomes. *IEEE Transactions on Engineering Management, 52*(1), 59-68.

Lingle, J. H., & Schiemann, W. A. (1996). From balanced scorecard to strategic gauges: is measurement worth it? *Management Review, 85*(3), 56-61.

Liu, L., Ratnatunga, J., & J. Yao, L. (2014). Firm characteristics and balanced scorecard usage in Singaporean manufacturing firms. *International Journal of Accounting & Information Management, 22*(3), 209-222.

Lonbani, M., Sofian, S., & Barato, M. B. (2014). *Review of using Balanced Scorecard among SMEs*. In International Management Accounting Conference (Vol. 7).

Lueg, R., & Vu, L. (2015). Success factors in Balanced Scorecard implementations–A literature review. *Management Revue,* 306-327.

Luo, X., Zhou, L., & Liu, S. S. (2005). Entrepreneurial firms in the context of China's transition economy: an integrative framework and empirical examination. *Journal of Business Research, 58*(3), 277-284.

Luther, R. G., & Longden, S. (2001). Management accounting in companies adapting to structural change and volatility in transition economies: a South African study. *Management Accounting Research, 12*(3), 299-320.

Luu, T. T. (2010). Balanced scorecard implementation at Rang Dong plastic joint-stock company (RDP). *Management Science and Engineering, 4*(2), 92.

Lybaert, N. (1998). The information use in a SME: Its importance and some elements of influence. *Small Business Economics, 10*(2), 171-191.

Maas, K., Schaltegger, S., & Crutzen, N. (2016). Integrating corporate sustainability assessment, management accounting, control, and reporting. *Journal of Cleaner Production, 136*, 237-248.

Mackenzie, N., & Knipe, S. (2006). Research dilemmas: Paradigms, methods and methodology. *Issues in Educational Research, 16*(2), 193-205.

Madsen, D. Ø. (2015). The Balanced Scorecard in the context of SMEs: A literature review. *Review of Business Research, 15*(3), 75-86.

Madsen, D. Ø., & Stenheim, T. (2015). The balanced scorecard: A review of five research areas. *American Journal of Management, 15*(2), 24-41.

Magdy Abdel-Kader, Souad Moufty, & Laitinen, a. E. K. (2011). Balanced Scorecard development. A Review of literature and directions for future research. In Magdy Abdel-Kader (Ed.), *Review of Management Accounting Research* (pp. 214-239). Basingstoke: Palgrave Macmillan.

Maiga, A. S., & Jacobs, F. A. (2003). Balanced scorecard, activity-based costing and company performance: an empirical analysis. *Journal of Managerial Issues, 15*(3), 283-301.

Maisel, L. S. (1992). Performance measurement: the balanced scorecard approach. *Journal of Cost Management, 6*(2), 47-52.

Major, E., & Cordey-Hayes, M. (2000). Engaging the business support network to give SMEs the benefit of foresight. *Technovation, 20*(11), 589-602.

Malagueño, R., Lopez-Valeiras, E., & Gomez-Conde, J. (2018). Balanced scorecard in SMEs: Effects on innovation and financial performance.

Small Business Economics, 51(1), 221-244.

Malmi, T. (2001). Balanced scorecards in Finnish companies: a research note. *Management Accounting Research, 12*(2), 207-220.

Manville, G. (2007). Implementing a balanced scorecard framework in a not for profit SME. *International Journal of Productivity and Performance Management, 56*(2), 162-169.

Marr, B., & Schiuma, G. (2003). Business performance measurement–past, present and future. *Management Decision, 41*(8), 680-687.

Marri, H., Gunasekaran, A., & Grieve, R. (2000). Performance measurements in the implementation of CIM in small and medium enterprises: an empirical analysis. *International Journal of Production Research, 38*(17), 4403-4411.

Marshall, J. P., Sorenson, R., Brigham, K., Wieling, E., Reifman, A., & Wampler, R. S. (2006). The paradox for the family firm CEO: Owner age relationship to succession-related processes and plans. *Journal of Business Venturing, 21*(3), 348-368.

Maruichi, D., & Abe, M. (2018). Corruption and the business environment in Viet Nam: An exploratory survey. In: ARTNeT Working Paper Series.

Mascarenhas, B. (1989). Domains of state-owned, privately held, and publicly traded firms in international competition. *Administrative Science Quarterly, 34*(4), 582-597.

Mathison, S. (1988). Why triangulate? *Educational Researcher, 17*(2), 13-17.

McAdam, R. (2000). Quality models in an SME context: a critical perspective using a grounded approach. *International Journal of Quality & Reliability Management, 17*(3), 305-323.

McCunn, P. (1998). The Balanced Scorecard... the eleventh commandment. *Management Accounting: Magazine for Chartered Management Accountants, 76*(11), 34-36.

McIntyre, R. J. (2003). Small enterprises in transition economies: causal puzzles and policy-relevant research. In R. J. McIntyre & B. Dallago (Eds.), *Small and Medium Enterprises in transitional economies* (pp. 1-18): Palgrave Macmillan.

McQuitty, S. (2004). Statistical power and structural equation models in business research. *Journal of Business Research, 57*(2), 175-183.

Mehralian, G., Nazari, J. A., Nooriparto, G., & Rasekh, H. R. (2017). TQM and organizational performance using the balanced scorecard approach. *International Journal of Productivity and Performance Management, 66*(1), 111-125.

Merchant, K. A. (1981). The design of the corporate budgeting system: influences on managerial behavior and performance. *The Accounting Review, 56*(4), 813-829.

Meyer, K. E., & Nguyen, H. V. (2005). Foreign investment strategies and sub-national institutions in emerging markets: Evidence from Vietnam. *Journal of Management Studies, 42*(1), 63-93.

Meyer, K. E., Tran, Y. T. T., & Nguyen, H. V. (2006). Doing business in Vietnam. *Thunderbird International Business Review, 48*(2), 263-290.

Mia, L., & Clarke, B. (1999). Market competition, management accounting systems and business unit performance. *Management Accounting Research, 10*(2), 137-158.

Möller, K., Partanen, J., Rajala, A., Westerlund, M., Rajala, R., & Svahn, S. (2005). *Role of partnerships and networks in SME innovation and growth.* Paper presented at the Proceedings of the IMP Conference, Rotterdam, The Netherlands.

Mooraj, S., Oyon, D., & Hostettler, D. (1999). The balanced scorecard: A necessary good or an unnecessary evil? *European Management Journal, 17*(5), 481-491.

Morgan, D. L. (2007). Paradigms lost and pragmatism regained: Methodological implications of combining qualitative and quantitative methods. *Journal of Mixed Methods Research, 1*(1), 48-76.

Moullin, M. (2003). Defining performance measurement. *Perspectives on Performance, 2*(2), 3.

Mukhtar, S.-M. (2002). Differences in male and female management characteristics: A study of owner-manager businesses. *Small Business Economics, 18*(4), 289-310.

Muli, K. G. (2016). *Extent of Balanced Scorecard implementation and its effect on the financial performance of Small and Medium enterprises in Nairobi Country.* (Master Book). University of Nairobi.

Munir Ahmad, M., & Alaskari, O. (2014). Development of assessment methodology for improving performance in SME's. *International Journal of Productivity and Performance Management, 63*(4), 477-498.

Murphy, G. D., & Southey, G. (2003). High performance work practices:

Perceived determinants of adoption and the role of the HR practitioner. *Personnel Review, 32*(1), 73-92.

Neely, A. (2005). The evolution of performance measurement research: Developments in the last decade and a research agenda for the next. *International Journal of Operations & Production Management, 25*(12), 1264-1277.

Neely, A., Gregory, M., & Platts, K. (1995). Performance measurement system design: A literature review and research agenda. *International Journal of Operations & Production Management, 15*(4), 80-116.

Nguyen, B., Mickiewicz, T., & Du, J. (2018). Local governance and business performance in Vietnam: the transaction costs' perspective. *Regional Studies, 52*(4), 542-557.

Nguyen, D. T., & Nguyen, T. M. T. (2009). *Nghiên cứu khoa học trong quản trị kinh doanh*: Thống kê.

Nguyen, L. (2018). *Management innovation: Case study of Balanced Scorecard implementation in Vietnam.* (PhD). University of Minnesota, (http://hdl.handle.net/11299/201134.)

Nguyen, T. T. H. (2016). *Small and medium-sized enterprises and sustainable development: the case of Vietnam.* (PhD). RMIT University,

Nguyen, T. T. N. (2017). The balanced scorecard application into the small and medium enterprises – Look at from the world's experience. *Journal of Science, Thu Dau Mot University, 2*(33), 116-119.

Niven, P. R. (2008). *Balanced scorecard: Step-by-step for government and nonprofit agencies*: John Wiley & Sons.

Niven, P. R. (2011). *Balanced scorecard: Step-by-step for government and nonprofit agencies*: John Wiley & Sons.

Noci, G. (1995). Accounting and non-accounting measures of quality-based performances in small firms. *International Journal of Operations & Production Management, 15*(7), 78-105.

Norreklit, H. (2000). The balance on the balanced scorecard a critical analysis of some of its assumptions. *Management Accounting Research, 11*(1), 65-88.

Nørreklit, H. (2003). The balanced scorecard: what is the score? A rhetorical analysis of the balanced scorecard. *Accounting, Organizations and Society, 28*(6), 591-619.

Norton, D. P., & Kaplan, R. S. (1993). Putting the balanced scorecard to work. *Harvard Business Review, 71*(5), 134-140.

Nunnally, J. C. (1978). *Psychometric Theory: 2d Ed*: McGraw-Hill.

Nyang'au, J. N. (2017). Application of the balanced Scorecard on change management and performance of commercial banks listed in the Nairobi Securities Exchange. In: Research project, University of Nairobi, Master of Business Administration ....

O'Regan, N., Sims, M., & Ghobadian, A. (2005). High performance: ownership and decision-making in SMEs. *Management Decision, 43*(3), 382-396.

Oghuvwu, M. E., & Omoye, A. (2016). Determinants of Balanced Scorecard Adoption: A Review of Perspectives. 1-11.

Oppenheim, A. N. (1992). *Questionnaire design: Interviewing and attitude measurement*. London: Pinter.

Osborne, J. W., Costello, A. B., & Kellow, J. T. (2008). Best practices in exploratory factor analysis. In J. Osborne (Ed.), *Best practices in quantitative methods* (pp. 86-99): Sage.

Otley, D. (1980). The contingency theory of management accounting: achievement and prognosis. In *Readings in accounting for management control* (pp. 83-106): Springer.

Otley, D. (1980). The contingency theory of management accounting: achievement and prognosis. *Accounting, Organizations and Society, 5*(4), 413-428.

Otley, D. (1999). Performance management: a framework for management control systems research. *Management Accounting Research, 10*(4), 363-382.

Otley, D. (2016). The contingency theory of management accounting and control: 1980–2014. *Management Accounting Research, 31*, 45-62.

Papadakis, V. M., Lioukas, S., & Chambers, D. (1998). Strategic decision-making processes: the role of management and context. *Strategic Management Journal, 19*(2), 115-147.

Patton, M. (1990). Purposeful sampling. *Qualitative Evaluation and Research Methods, 2*, 169-186.

Pekkola, S., Saunila, M., & Rantanen, H. (2016). Performance measurement system implementation in a turbulent operating environment. *International Journal of Productivity and Performance Management, 65*(7), 947-958.

Peña, E. D. (2007). Lost in translation: Methodological considerations in cross-cultural research. *Child Development, 78*(4), 1255-1264.

Peng, M. W., Tan, J., & Tong, T. W. (2004). Ownership types and strategic groups in an emerging economy. *Journal of Management Studies, 41*(7), 1105-1129.

Perera, S., Schoch, H., & Sabaratnam, S. (2007). Adoption of the Balanced Scorecard in Local Government Organizations: An exploratory study. *Asia-Pacific Management Accounting Journal,* 2(1), 53-70.

Peterson, R. A. (1994). A meta-analysis of Cronbach's coefficient alpha. *Journal of Consumer Research, 21*(2), 381-391.

Phadtare, M. T. (2010). Developing Balanced Scorecard: Case of three construction firms of small size. *Journal of Asia-Pacific Business, 11*(2), 135-157.

Pham, D. H. (2017). *Credit Access, Networks, Institutions and Performance of Small and Medium-Sized Enterprises: Insights from Vietnam.* Georg-August-Universität Göttingen,

Pham, H. C., & Bui, V. M. (2015). The present of Balanced scorecard application in Small and Medium enterprises in Ho Chi Minh City, Vietnam. *Journal of Science, An Giang University,* 3(2), 85 - 92.

Phan, T. X. H. (2017). *Building a BSC for Khanh Hoa's Aquatic product processing enterprises.* (Master of Business Administration). Da Nang

Phillips, B., Wee, T. T. T., & Shanka, T. (2003). The use of performance measures in small and medium enterprises (SMEs)–an exploratory study. In: Curtin Business School, Australia, .

Phuong, N. T., Fisher, G., & Mujtaba, B. G. (2014). Ethical decision-making of banking and finance professionals and students. *Asian Journal of Business Ethics,* 3(2), 141-153.

Piercy, K. W. (2004). Analysis of semi-structured interview data. In. Logan, Utah: Department of Family, Consumer, & Human Development, Utah State University, .

Premaratne, S. P. (2001). Networks, resources, and small business growth: The experience in Sri Lanka. *Journal of Small Business Management, 39*(4), 363-371.

Quesado, P. R., Aibar-Guzmán, B., & Rodrigues, L. L. (2014). Determinant Factors of the Implementation of the Balanced Scorecard in Portugal: Empirical evidence in public and private organizations. *Revista Brasileira de Gestão de Negócios, 16*(51), 199-222.

Quesado, P. R., Aibar-Guzmán, B., & Rodrigues, L. L. (2016). Extrinsic and intrinsic factors in the balanced scorecard adoption: an empirical study in Portuguese organizations. *European Journal of Management and Business Economics, 25*(2), 47-55.

Quinn Patton, M. (2002). *Qualitative research and evaluation methods*: Sage.

Rababah, A. (2015). The relationship between cultural factors and balanced scorecard implementation. *International Review of Management and Business Research, 4*(4), 1208-1218.

Radnor, Z., & Lovell, B. (2003). Success factors for implementation of the balanced scorecard in a NHS multi-agency setting. *International Journal of Health Care Quality Assurance, 16*(2), 99-108.

Ralston, D. A., Van Thang, N., & Napier, N. K. (1999). A comparative study of the work values of North and South Vietnamese managers. *Journal of International Business Studies, 30*(4), 655-672.

Rantanen, H., Kulmala, H. I., Lönnqvist, A., & Kujansivu, P. (2007). Performance measurement systems in the Finnish public sector. *International Journal of Public Sector Management, 20*(5), 415-433.

Rauch, A., Wiklund, J., Lumpkin, G. T., & Frese, M. (2009). Entrepreneurial orientation and business performance: An assessment of past research and suggestions for the future. *Entrepreneurship Theory and Practice, 33*(3), 761-787.

Reefke, H., & Trocchi, M. (2013). Balanced scorecard for sustainable supply chains: Design and development guidelines. *International Journal of Productivity and Performance Management, 62*(8), 805-826.

Richard, P. J., Devinney, T. M., Yip, G. S., & Johnson, G. (2009). Measuring organizational performance: Towards methodological best practice. *Journal of Management, 35*(3), 718-804.

Riedel, J., & Comer, B. (1997). Transition to a market economy in Vietnam. *Economies in Transition: Comparing Asia and Eastern Europe*, 189-213.

Rigby, D., & Bilodeau, B. (2009). *Management tools & trends*. Boston, MA: Bain & Company

Rigby, D., & Bilodeau, B. (2011). *Management tools & trends*. Boston, MA: Bain & Company

Rigby, D., & Bilodeau, B. (2013). *Management tools & trends*. Boston, MA: Bain & Company.

Rigby, D., & Bilodeau, B. (2015). *Management tools & trends*. Boston, MA: Bain & Company.

Robbins, S. P. (2006). *Organizational behavior* (2nd ed.). South Africa: Pearson.

Robson, C. (1993). Interviews and questionnaires. In C. Robson (Ed.), *Real World Research* (pp. 227-243). Oxford, UK: Blackwell.

Rodríguez, A. C., Molina, M. A., Pérez, A. L. G., & Hernández, U. M. (2003). Size, age and activity sector on the growth of the small and medium firm size. *Small Business Economics, 21*(3), 289-307.

Rogers, E. M. (1995). Diffusion of Innovations: Modifications of a model for telecommunications. In M.-W. Stoetzer & A. Mahler (Eds.), *Die diffusion von innovationen in der telekommunikation* (pp. 25-38): Springer.

Rompho, N. (2011). Why the balanced scorecard fails in SMEs: A case study. *International Journal of Business and Management, 6*(11), 39-46.

Rosenbusch, N., Brinckmann, J., & Bausch, A. (2011). Is innovation always beneficial? A meta-analysis of the relationship between innovation and performance in SMEs. *Journal of business Venturing, 26*(4), 441-457.

Rowe, F., Truex, D., & Huynh, M. Q. (2012). An empirical study of determinants of e-commerce adoption in SMEs in Vietnam: An economy in transition. *Journal of Global Information Management (JGIM), 20*(3), 23-54.

Roxas, H. B. G., Lindsay, V., Ashill, N., & Victorio, A. (2009). Economic accountability in the context of local governance in the Philippines: A structural equation modelling approach. *Asia Pacific Journal of Public Administration, 31*(1), 17-37.

Ryan, G. W., & Bernard, H. R. (2000). Data management and analysis methods. In N. Densin & Y. Loncoln (Eds.), *Handbook of Qualitative Research* (pp. 769-802). Thousand Oaks, CA: Sage.

Santagada, G. (2012). Using Balanced Scorecard to drive performance in Small and Medium Enterprises. *Ekonomika a Management, 2012*(1), 15-27.

Santarelli, E., & Tran, H. T. (2016). Diversification strategies and firm performance in Vietnam: Evidence from parametric and semi-parametric approaches. *Economics of Transition, 24*(1), 31-68.

Sartor, M. (2019). The Balanced Scorecard. In M. Sartor & G. Orzes (Eds.), *Quality management: Tools, methods, and standards.* (pp. 55-76): Emerald Publishing.

Saunders, B., Elliott-Sale, K., Artioli, G. G., Swinton, P. A., Dolan, E., Roschel, H., . . . Gualano, B. (2017). β-alanine supplementation to improve exercise capacity and performance: a systematic review and meta-analysis. *British Journal of Sports Medicine, 51*(8), 658-669.

Saunila, M. (2016). Performance measurement approach for innovation capability in SMEs. *International Journal of Productivity and Performance Management, 65*(2), 162-176.

Schlevogt, K.-A. (2001). Institutional and organizational factors affecting effectiveness: Geoeconomic comparison between Shanghai and Beijing. *Asia Pacific Journal of Management, 18*(4), 519-551.

Schmiedel, T., Vom Brocke, J., & Recker, J. (2014). Development and validation of an instrument to measure organizational cultures' support of Business Process Management. *Information & Management, 51*(1), 43-56.

Schwandt, T. A. (1997). *Qualitative inquiry: A dictionary of terms*: Sage Publications, Inc.

Scotland, J. (2012). Exploring the philosophical underpinnings of research: Relating ontology and epistemology to the methodology and methods of the scientific, interpretive, and critical research paradigms. *English Language Teaching, 5*(9), 9-16.

Scott, D., & Usher, R. (2010). *Researching education: Data, methods and theory in educational enquiry*: Bloomsbury Publishing.

Sekaran, U., & Bougie, R. (1992). *Research method for business. A skill building approach.* . New York: John Wiley & Sons.

Sekaran, U., & Bougie, R. (2003). *Research methods for business. A skill building approach* New York: John Wiley & Sons.

Shahin Firoozmand, Philip Haxel, Euijin Jung, & Suomien, a. K. (2015). *Report of State of SME finance in the United States in 2015.*

Sharma, M. K., & Bhagwat, R. (2006). Performance measurements in the implementation of information systems in small and medium-sized enterprises: A framework and empirical analysis. *Measuring Business Excellence, 10*(4), 8-21.

Sidani, Y., & Al Ariss, A. (2014). Institutional and corporate drivers of global talent management: Evidence from the Arab Gulf region. *Journal of World Business, 49*(2), 215-224.

Sila, I. (2007). Examining the effects of contextual factors on TQM and performance through the lens of organizational theories: An empirical study. *Journal of Operations management, 25*(1), 83-109.

Simons, R. (1990). Rethinking the role of systems in controlling strategy. *Harvard Business School Teaching Notes*, 9-91.

Simpson, M., Tuck, N., & Bellamy, S. (2004). Small business success factors: The role of education and training. *Education+ Training, 46*(8/9), 481-491.

Singh, R. K., & Arora, S. S. (2018). The adoption of balanced scorecard: An exploration of its antecedents and consequences. *Benchmarking: An International Journal, 25*(3), 874-892.

Smith, G. (2010). *Performance measurement systems and performance measures: The good, the bad and the ugly*. Paper presented at the Australasian Evaluation Society Conference Wellington New Zealand.

Sondakh, O. (2015). The effect of strategic management BSC on micro enterprises' (MIES) business performance in Surabaya – Indonesia with intellectual capital as an intervening variable. *Internatioinal Journal of Applied Business and Economic Research, 13*(7), 4647 - 4657.

Sondakh, O., Budiman, C., & Ellitan, L. (2017). Measuring organizational performance: A case study of food industry SMEs in Surabaya-Indonesia. *International Journal of Scientific Research and Management, 5*(12), 7681-7689.

Sorooshian, S., Aziz, N. F., Ahmad, A., Jubidin, S. N., & Mustapha, N. M. (2016). Review on Performance Measurement Systems. *Mediterranean Journal of Social Sciences, 7*(1), 123-132.

Speckbacher, G., Bischof, J., & Pfeiffer, T. (2003). A descriptive analysis on the implementation of balanced scorecards in German-speaking countries. *Management Accounting Research, 14*(4), 361-388.

Suprapto, B., Wahab, H. A., & Wibowo, A. J. (2012). The implementation of Balance Score Card for performance measurement in Small and Medium Enterprises: Evidence from Malaysian health care services. *The Asian Journal of Technology Management, 2*(2), 76-87.

Swierczek, F. W., & Thai, T. H. (2003). Motivation, entrepreneurship and the performance of SMEs in Vietnam. *Journal of Enterprising Culture, 11*(01), 47-68.

Ta, L. N. H. (2019). *Factors affecting the application of the Balanced Scorecard to Small and Medium-sized Enterprises in Ho Chi Minh City.*

Tabachnick, B. G., & Fidell, L. S. (1996). *Using multivariate statistics* (3rd ed.). New York: Harper Collins.

Tashakkori, A., Teddlie, C., & Teddlie, C. B. (1998). *Mixed methodology: Combining qualitative and quantitative approaches* (Vol. 46): Sage.

Taticchi, P., Balachandran, K., Botarelli, M., & Cagnazzo, L. (2008). Performance measurement management for small and medium enterprises: An integrated approach. *Journal of Applied Management Accounting Research, 6*(2), 57-72.

Taticchi, P., Tonelli, F., & Cagnazzo, L. (2010). Performance measurement and management: A literature review and a research agenda. *Measuring Business Excellence, 14*(1), 4 - 18.

Taylor, A., & Taylor, M. (2014). Factors influencing effective implementation of performance measurement systems in small and medium-sized enterprises and large firms: A perspective from Contingency Theory. *International Journal of Production Research, 52*(3), 847-866.

Teddlie, C., & Tashakkori, A. (2009). *Foundations of mixed methods research: Integrating quantitative and qualitative approaches in the social and behavioral sciences*: Sage.

Tenev, S., Carlier, A., Chaudry, O., & Nguyen, Q.-T. (2003). *Informality and the playing field in Vietnam's business sector*: World Bank Publications.

Tennant, C., & Tanoren, M. (2005). Performance management in SMEs: A Balanced Scorecard perspective. *International Journal of Business Performance Management, 7*(2), 123-143.

Thakkar, J., Kanda, A., & Deshmukh, S. (2009). Supply chain performance measurement framework for small and medium scale enterprises. *Benchmarking: An International Journal, 16*(5), 702-723.

Thompson, B. (2004). *Exploratory and confirmatory factor analysis: Understanding concepts and applications*: American Psychological Association.

Thong, J. Y., & Yap, C.-S. (1995). CEO characteristics, organizational characteristics and information technology adoption in small businesses. *Omega, 23*(4), 429-442.

Thornton, G. (2019). *Women in business: Building a blueprint for action*. Retrieved from https://www.grantthornton.global/globalassets/global-insights---do-not-edit/2019/women-in-business/gtil-wib-report_grant-thornton-spreads-low-res.pdf

Tran, H. T. T. (2015). Challenges of Small and Medium-Sized Enterprises (SMEs) In Vietnam during the process of integration into the ASEAN Economic Community (AEC). *International Journal of Accounting and Financial Reporting, 5*(2), 133-143.

Tran, Q. T., & Vu, V. H. (2018). The impact of government support on innovations of Small and Medium Enterprises in Vietnam. *VNU Journal of*

Science: Economics and Business, 34(4).

Tran, Q. V. (2012). *Factors influencing the adoption level of Balanced Scorecard in strategic management of enterprises in Vietnam.* (PhD). Institute for Business Managgement Studies and Applications.

Tran, T. B., Grafton, R. Q., & Kompas, T. (2009). Institutions matter: The case of Vietnam. *The Journal of Socio-Economics, 38*(1), 1-12.

Tran, T. C., Le, X. S., & Nguyen, K. A. (2007). *Vietnam's small and medium sized enterprises development: Characteristics, constraints and policy recommendations.* Retrieved from http://www.eria.org/Vietnam%E2%80%99s%20 Small%20and%20Medium%20Sized%

Tran, T. C., Sang, L., & Anh, N. (2007). *Vietnam's small and medium sized enterprises development: Characteristics, constraints and policy recommendations.* Retrieved from http://www.eria.org/Vietnam%E2%80%99s%20 Small%20and%20Medium%20Sized%

Tran, T. H. *Determinants of innovative decision of Vietnamese Small and Medium-sized Enterprises.* Paper presented at the Proceedings of the International Academic Research Conference on Small & Medium Enterprises(SMEs), Vietnam, Hanoi.

Tran, V. H., & Charles, H. (2016). *New Asian regionalism: responses to globalisation and crises*: Springer.

Tran, X. L. (2013). to explore the possibility of BSC adoption in construction SMEs in Vietnam.

Trinh, T. A. (2014). Implementation of balanced scorecard in Vietnamese enteprises. *Journal of Science Ho Chi Minh City Open University,* 4(12), 67-74.

Van Teijlingen, E. R., & Hundley, V. (2001). The importance of pilot studies.

Venkatraman, N., & Ramanujam, V. (1986). Measurement of business performance in strategy research: A comparison of approaches. *Academy of Management Review, 11*(4), 801-814.

Vo, V. D. (2015). The effects of local business environments on SMEs' performance: Empirical evidence from the Mekong Delta. *Asian Academy of Management Journal, 20*(1).

Vo, V. N., & Pham, N. T. (2018). *Factors influencing to the application of Balanced Scorecard among listed companies in Ho Chi Minh.* Paper presented at the The 5th IBSM International Conference on Business, Management and Accounting 19-21 April 2018. Hanoi University of Industry, Vietnam.

Voelker, K. E., Rakich, J. S., & French, G. R. (2001). The balanced scorecard in healthcare organizations: a performance measurement and strategic planning methodology. *Hospital Topics, 79*(3), 13-24.

Volery, T., Mueller, S., & von Siemens, B. (2015). Entrepreneur ambidexterity: A study of entrepreneur behaviours and competencies in growth-oriented small and medium-sized enterprises. *International Small Business Journal, 33*(2), 109-129.

Von Bergen, C., & Benco, D. C. (2004). *A balanced scorecard for small business.* Paper presented at the Proceedings of the United States Association for Small Business and Entrepreneurship Conference. Dallas, Texas.

Vu, T. K. A., Vu, T. D., & Hoang, K. V. (2018). Using the Balanced Scorecard to measure the performance of Small and Medium- Sized garment enterprises in Vietnam. *Accounting and Finance Research, Vol. 7, No. 3; 2018.*

Vuong, K. T. (2018). Analysis of managerial factors on the performance of Small and Medium-sized enterprises in manufacturing sector in Ho Chi Minh-Vietnam. *British Journal of Marketing Studies, 6*(1), 26-51.

Vuong, Q. H. (2014). Vietnam's political economy in transition (1986-2016). *Stratfor-The Hub: International Perspectives.* Retrieved from https://worldview.stratfor.com/article/vietnams-political-economy-transition-1986-2016

Vuong, T. T., Semerák, V., & Vuong, Q. H. (2019). The Vietnamese economy at the crossroads. In *Southeast Asia and the ASEAN Economic Community* (pp. 91-143): Springer.

Walker, E., & Brown, A. (2004). What success factors are important to small business owners? *International Small Business Journal, 22*(6), 577-594.

Wan, D., Ong, C. H., & Lee, F. (2005). Determinants of firm innovation in Singapore. *Technovation, 25*(3), 261-268.

Wang, M. (2016). *Issues of Balanced Scorecard and Its Implication for Chinese Companies.* Auckland University of Technology,

Wang, R., & Gu, H. (2016). *Determinant factors influencing the use of Balanced Scorecard in China.* (Master). Uppsala,

Wang, W.-L., Lee, H.-L., & Fetzer, S. J. (2006). Challenges and strategies of instrument translation. *Western Journal of Nursing Research, 28*(3), 310-321.

Wanguku, A. K. (2013). *Adoption of the Balanced Scorecard as a strategic approach by large international non-governmental organizations in Kenya.* (MBA). University of Nairobi,

Waring, T., & Wainwright, D. (2008). Issues and challenges in the use of template analysis: Two comparative case studies from the field. *Electronic Journal of Business Research Methods, 6*(1).

Watson, J., & Robinson, S. (2003). Adjusting for risk in comparing the performances of male-and female-controlled SMEs. *Journal of Business Venturing, 18*(6), 773-788.

Watts, T., & McNair-Connolly, C. J. (2012). New performance measurement and management control systems. *Journal of Applied Accounting Research, 13*(3), 226-241.

Widener, S. K. (2006). Associations between strategic resource importance and performance measure use: The impact on firm performance. *Management Accounting Research, 17*(4), 433-457.

Woodward, J. (1980). *Industrial organization; theory and practice*: Oxford University Press.

World Bank. (2015). Small and medium enterprises finance report 1/2015.

Wu, D. (2009). *Measuring performance in small and medium enterprises in the information and communication technology industries.* (PhD). RMIT University.

Wu, L., & Chang, C.-H. (2012). Using the balanced scorecard in assessing the performance of e-SCM diffusion: A multi-stage perspective. *Decision Support Systems, 52*(2), 474-485.

Yadav, N., & Sagar, M. (2013). Performance measurement and management frameworks: Research trends of the last two decades. *Business Process Management Journal, 19*(6), 947-971.

Yang, J., & Jiehui, L. (2005). A framework for applying Balanced Scorecard to Chinese SMEs.

Yusuf, A. (1995). Critical success factors for small business: Perceptions of South Pacific entrepreneurs. *Journal of Small Business Management, 33*(2), 68-73.

Zain, M., & Ng, S. I. (2006). The impacts of network relationships on SMEs' internationalization process. *Thunderbird International Business Review, 48*(2), 183-205.

Zikmund, W. G. (2003). *Business research methods*: Thomson South-Western

Zuriekat, M. I. K. (2005). *Performance measurement systems: An examination of the influence of the contextual factors and their impact on performance with a specific emphasis on the balanced scorecard approach.* University of Huddersfield.

www.ingramcontent.com/pod-product-compliance
Lightning Source LLC
LaVergne TN
LVHW101504200926
848483LV00001B/223
* 9 7 8 1 8 0 4 4 1 2 7 2 5 *